"David Sliker is a man who has poured out his life prayerfully studying the end of this age. This is not a book of popular end-times sensationalism; it is a fountain of genuine apostolic wisdom for all with ears to hear and eyes to see what is coming."

Joel Richardson, *New York Times* bestselling author and speaker

"David has been always a very insightful student and teacher of the Word, especially concerning the end times. *The Nations Rage* is going to make you love Jesus' leadership more and see the world system with the right eyes. We truly need books like this that—together with our daily meditation and revelation of the Word of God—will allow us to respond well, as churches, leaders and families, to the return of our Beloved, which is drawing near."

Netz Gómez, senior pastor, Houses of Light Church; founder, Northridge House of Prayer

"My friend David Sliker is one of the brightest minds today when it comes to end-time prophecy. Behold the drama of God's glory poured on the Church, nations revolting against it and God's judgment of their rebellion. Knowing where He's taking us will give you the courage to live wholeheartedly for Him today."

Bob Sorge, author, *Secrets of the Secret Place*

"I believe that Psalm 2 is one of the most important chapters in the Word of God for this hour. In *The Nations Rage*, my friend David Sliker has pressed this psalm on us to consider and to humbly respond to accordingly. We are moving into the most glorious and intense hour of human history, and we need help preparing our hearts and minds so that we may respond rightly. I've known and labored with David Sliker for over fifteen years, and I believe that this book, if read on your knees, can literally alter your life and prepare you for this next season."

Corey Russell, author and conference speaker

"Resist the temptation to think this is just another book telling you how corrupted society has become. Honestly, I don't need to be told yet again that things are falling apart. What I need, and have found in this excellent new book, is a biblical analysis of what will happen in the days ahead. With penetrating insight into our current circumstances and the promises of God's Word concerning the future, Sliker charts a course forward. Regardless of your personal views on biblical eschatology, Sliker will challenge you to reexamine your expectations of what is coming to the world in advance of the coming of Christ the King."

Dr. Sam Storms, lead pastor of preaching and vision,
Bridgeway Church

"One of the most neglected themes in our pulpits today is the return of the Lord Jesus and the global conditions that will precede it. In *The Nations Rage*, David Sliker takes the reader on a journey, giving clarity about the seriousness of that hour and confidence in heaven's response. I highly recommend this book to anyone whose heart cries, '*Maranatha!*'"

Lee M. Cummings, senior pastor, Radiant Church;
founder, Radiant Network;
author, *Be Radiant* and *Flourish*

"This is a serious book about a serious subject written by a serious student of the Word. While we cannot set dates for the Lord's return, we know that we are living in urgent times, and this book is designed to equip you to be a truth-based, Spirit-empowered overcomer."

Dr. Michael L. Brown, host, *The Line of Fire* radio broadcast;
author, *Jezebel's War with America*

"David Sliker carries a message about Jesus and the coming days that this generation needs. I have watched him walk with integrity and devotedness to his wife and family in such a way that these words on a public page have their standing in private. David loves the God of whom he writes, and his passion is for God's name and His glory. David consistently challenges the comfortable and comforts the broken—much like the Jesus to whom he points us."

Sara E. Hagerty, bestselling author, *Every Bitter Thing Is Sweet*,
Unseen, and *Adore*

"Some call it a conspiracy theory. My friend David Sliker calls it biblical prophecy. Dark, sinister forces are even now galvanizing under the guise of human progress and driving toward a globalist world in rebellion against God. God and His Church stand as the one obstacle to their collusion. Thus, the final rage of Satan against the Lord and His anointed. Read this book, prepare spiritually for the days that are rushing upon us and be a part of that glorified Church that overcomes at the end of the age."

Lou Engle, president, Lou Engle Ministries; co-founder, TheCall

David Sliker has been a dear friend of mine for more than a decade. He is one of the most bold, dedicated and passionate men of this generation. I am grateful for his commitment to the advancement of the Kingdom and glory of God. I have watched him study the Word of God, not just for information, but to know the man Jesus Christ. I know his heart for the Church to encounter the beauty of God, displayed through His end-time plan and judgments, is sincere and deeply rooted in love. I believe as you read these words and glean from David's many hours of study and prayer, your heart will be awakened to the beauty and knowledge of God.

Brian Kim, founder, Antioch Center for Training and Sending

"David Sliker has given many years of study, prayer and sound instruction to a subject often neglected but of critical importance for the Body of Christ—the beauty of Jesus as Bridegroom, King and Judge. I recommend David as someone who I trust to faithfully present this message. He is a man who cares about rightly and carefully dividing the Word of God with a spirit of love and humility. I am thankful for David and his family, who have labored diligently to live this message well over a sustained period of time."

Mike Bickle, director, International House of Prayer of Kanas City

THE
NATIONS
RAGE

PRAYER, PROMISE AND POWER
IN AN ANTI-CHRISTIAN AGE

DAVID SLIKER

Chosen

a division of Baker Publishing Group
Minneapolis, Minnesota

© 2020 by David Sliker

Published by Chosen Books
11400 Hampshire Avenue South
Bloomington, Minnesota 55438
www.chosenbooks.com

Chosen Books is a division of
Baker Publishing Group, Grand Rapids, Michigan

Printed in the United States of America

ISBN 978-0-8007-6192-9 (trade paper)
ISBN 978-0-8007-6220-9 (casebound)

Cover design by Rob Williams, InsideOutCreativeArts

20 21 22 23 24 25 26   7 6 5 4 3 2 1

To Tracey, my bride
For you and for our grandchildren,
so that in the days to come they might know
where we are going, how we got here
and what we need to do about it.

CONTENTS

Foreword by Mike Bickle   11

Introduction   15

Part One: The Church and the Coming Storm of Glory

1. Preparing to Engage in the Future Now   25

2. Divine Justice and the Return of Jesus   49

3. Three Storms That Will Change the World   69

4. The Coming Storm of Revival   83

5. The Coming Storm of Rage   101

6. The Coming Storm of Political and Economic Disruption   121

Part Two: The Church in an Anti-Christian Age

7. The Birth of the Cultural Narrative   137

8. The Modern Expression of the Cultural Narrative   161

Contents

Part Three: The Promise of the Victorious Church

9. The Way of Victory and Redemption   179

10. Preparing the Next Generation   195

11. Burning and Shining Lamps   213

12. Counted Worthy of This Calling   223

Notes   235

FOREWORD

I believe that the book you hold in your hands will be one of the most important books that you could read in this hour of history. In a time when many are focused on the present crises, financial pressures and personal disruptions, David Sliker has produced something that can help us set our eyes on the much greater problem that lies beyond the troubles of today. This problem involves the blazing purity, love and holiness of God as He seeks to fully engage with His Church and the lost world.

Many teachers speak of the kindness, mercy and compassion of the Lord toward us. I am grateful for this foundational message and for those who work hard to help people see the heart of love that Jesus possesses for people. What is also needed in this hour of history is a robust teaching on the fear of the Lord and His holiness alongside these messages of faith, hope and love. Isaiah spoke of being strengthened by cultivating a fear of God and a greater insight into the beauty of God: "Wisdom and knowledge will be the stability of your times, and the strength of salvation; the fear of the LORD is His treasure. . . . Your eyes will see the King in His beauty" (Isaiah 33:6, 17). More than ever, we need the whole counsel of God and the knowledge of Him that we might stand with unshakable confidence and great resolve even in the face of escalating pressure that is sure to come in the days ahead.

Modern people have given little thought to the dilemma associated with a holy God invading a broken, fallen, rebellious world. But we must wrestle with the disruptive dynamics of God's power, temporal judgments and zeal to remove everything that hinders His love across the world. Too rarely do we consider that God wants to do more than simply bless us now and evaluate our lives in the age to come. He desires not just to remove us to another world beyond the veil, but to invade and change the world we currently inhabit. The collision between holy and unholy—as a radiant, pure, undefiled God enters our sinful world—has serious consequences. To my knowledge, few have written on those consequences and even fewer are calling the Body of Christ to prepare for the coming collision of the two worlds.

I urge you, then, to read this book with special care and to take time to do so prayerfully. This is a book that needs to be considered beyond mere curiosity about the future and what it may hold. It contains truths that need to be reflected on and recommitted to when the race becomes difficult and we become weary in our "long obedience in the same direction," as Eugene Peterson once wrote.

I am thankful for David's work to bring this message forth for times such as these. I believe that, as strange and uncomfortable as the current pressures are, they are merely the beginning of even greater pressures to come in the years ahead. Therefore, it is vital that the Body of Christ live with urgency as we consider the events surrounding Jesus' return by cultivating spiritual strength in our inner lives now so that we can successfully navigate the future and thrive in the face of greater temptations and persecutions.

Therefore, this kind of book and teaching resource is essential in helping us connect ideas and passages in the Bible that we haven't focused on very much in the past. These ideas have always been in the Scriptures, but they make the most sense to the generation of the Lord's return, for as we draw nearer to the Lord's return, the prophetic Scriptures and God's redemptive story line will become clearer to us. The great gift of the Holy Spirit's leadership as the Teacher who will "guide you into all truth . . . and tell you things to come" is the gift of clarity (John 16:13). Clarity and understanding give us courage and resolve to press into the plans and purposes of God as the world becomes more uncertain and difficult to navigate. I encourage you to gain clarity on the end-time plan of God and to apprehend the courage and conviction that follow, leading to a lifestyle of prayer and fasting, the pursuit of holiness and a fear of the Lord—all things that equip us to enjoy our full destiny in Christ, together.

In that regard, we need a thousand books such as this one, with a thousand different voices from around the world giving leadership and clarity to the passion and purpose of Christ in these crucial years. My prayer is that yours would become one of those voices.

Mike Bickle, director, International House of Prayer
of Kanas City

INTRODUCTION

I t is not uncommon for Westerners, by and large, to think about the future in self-absorbed terms. Christians in the West sometimes do the same, using words such as destiny and calling and phrases like "being what I'm made to be," reducing the future to a canvas upon which to paint personal ambitions. Therefore, when we think about the future we may be merely dreaming up ways to escape the dreariness of our mundane lives rather than thinking along biblical lines. Much of modern Western Christianity can seem, at times, to be about looking for ways to improve circumstances and comfort. We do not want it to be this way. Thankfully, we have a God-given longing for eternity that causes us to ache for something more than the superficiality of the culture we are surrounded by. There is something deeper within us that desires the permanence of the age to come versus the sinful, broken construct of a world that is rapidly passing away.

Sadly (even as some export this superficial version of Christianity to the rest of the world), we may not realize that we have absorbed a cultural construct that is not helpful to us—one that strays from the biblical view of the world. The Bible does not promise a pain-free life or the end of all suffering. It never tells us that things will always be easy, or that our circumstances will always be happy during our time on this earth. Biblical self-fulfillment does not come from happy circumstances. God's blessings and favor do not match our culture's definition of the ideal life. If we cling to a culture of self-centered optimism disguised as a modern form of biblical hope, we will eventually find ourselves disillusioned and cynical, rolling our eyes with world-weary frustration at the sunny optimism of our misplaced idealism. In addition, we may become unable or unwilling to lean into the grace and help of the Holy Spirit that will be necessary in the difficult days to come. If we are not careful, our cultural, self-help-oriented positivism can initiate a very different conversation from the one the Father wants to have with us about the future.

It may never occur to most of us that this kind of self-centered thinking is a relatively new phenomenon in human history. Westerners are unusually blessed with abundance, even if we feel the pinch of the cost of living. The very fact that we dream about the cars we want to buy and the vacations we want to save for and the future houses we might purchase sets us apart from the vast majority of the human population that has gone before us. If past generations could behold our daily lives and ambitions, we would seem to them like people from another world.

Actually, the relative newness of our ambitious ideas should inform us that the ways in which we think about the future are not exactly biblical in nature or origin. For the most part, the people who populate the Bible grew up in one locality and followed their fathers' trades. They were oppressed by kings and empires with powerful militaries and concentrated wealth.

The Bible is for us, but it was not written initially to us, nor is it about us.

Yet it is more than likely that we find ourselves in the final generation before the Lord's return, the generation that the Bible speaks about often in context of the unique dynamics that surround His return. One could argue that many of our generation are practically incapable and emotionally unable to face these unique dynamics of trouble and glory with true faith and courage. Still there is much hope. The great cloud of witnesses that the writer of Hebrews spoke of, who watch the tireless labors of Jesus to bring His Church into the fullness of her destiny, will be astonished to see the final generation before the Lord's return—the one with so much working against it historically, politically, socially and emotionally—produce men and women of solid heavenly caliber. When we come to the absolute end of our own strength, gifts, abilities and resources, He is able to do breathtaking things to bring His people into the fullness of their true destiny. He is our hope, and the Bible is all about Him.

The Bible never talks about Jesus' aptitudes, gifts or abilities. We do not know what He could do in His own strength and natural talent, apart from carpentry that He learned from His father. We know much about Him from the Scriptures, yet in modern terms, we know nothing about Him. We do not know about His personality profile, His management aptitudes or His corporate leadership and productivity levels. My point here is not to call these approaches into question. I do not have a problem with these tools; they serve their purpose related to efficiency and team building. I am interested in the contrast between the secondary things that our culture elevates as the most important details and what the Bible actually describes. While gifts and personality profiles can help us to accomplish tasks, the Bible wants to emphasize something very different, and very powerful about the Man from Nazareth. What are we to know about Jesus?

We know that He was and is the ultimate Apostle, Prophet, Teacher, Evangelist, Shepherd and the rightful King of Israel. The Bible tells us mostly about His character, His attributes and attitudes, and what He was like in very human terms. We know Him best not as a gifted man, but as the Man of the Cross. We know most about how He loves. We know how He serves. We know that He is coming again. He is the ultimate expression of human potential, emptied of self, abandoned in fiery passion and love for His Bride. He is committed to bringing us into the same place with the same heart.

O, the Man of the Cross! The One who defined what it means to be truly human and fully alive displayed the beauty of human potential as His Father defined it. He was the One who did only what He saw the Father doing; he was fully yielded to the authority of His Father (John 5:18–20). The One who is seated as a man upon the highest seat of authority a human being can occupy is the Lamb who was slain. God brought the One who had utterly lowered Himself to the place of highest authority; the humblest man who ever lived was given the place of greatest power. That is one of the core themes of this book: power, and what it means in the light of the redemption of sinful, fallen humanity. The story of the great power struggle between God and humankind is an ancient story with a future climax. The fact that there is even a conflict at all between an eternal, infinite, omnipotent Creator and His mortal created beings tells us everything we need to know about His kindness, His mercy and His stunning humility. It also tells us why we want the conflict to end, that we might be with Him and enjoy Him in His fullness and glory forever.

I think about where we are today and how we arrived here. I consider what we believe and what it means for the future. And I think about how unprepared we are.

Whenever I look at the trajectory of history and the inevitable escalation of sin and darkness, glory and holiness, I remember the only way forward. I must look at Jesus far more than I do the world around me. The more I know and love Him, the greater my hope. The urgency of the hour requires that I cling to the things that really matter, the things that the Bible calls wise and worthy of my time and energy. In the meantime, I must stop justifying the trivial and meaningless arguments and discussions that fill my mind and compete for that same amount of attention.

How do I go about this?

I can discern the times (see Luke 12:56). I can discover that I live in days of false promise for a perpetually bright future, even when all evidence and human nature shout to the contrary. Far better than the cultural construct of positivism and the false gospel of bigger and better, the genuine beauty of Jesus enlists us in the lifelong fight to be with Him and to truly know Him, no matter the cost, the loss or the pain. This is authentic, historic Christianity.

What was it like for past generations when, in a moment, disease, war and trouble found its way to their door? Such a crisis must have drastically changed the way they spent their precious remaining moments, because a crisis quickly dispels the myth of having infinite time, the myth that we believe when we are young, ambitious and ignorant of our actual future. Living as we do under the umbrella of a cultural promise of a perpetual bright future (even when all evidence and human nature shout to the contrary), we are predisposed to positivism and the pursuit of comfort and ease, and squandering hours on things that have no significance or true eternal value. Yet Jesus loves us deeply and is fully committed to helping us out of our cultural dilemma and into His clear-sighted Kingdom of love and mercy and prayer.

I have very little influence over the larger world; my greatest impact lies in the life of Jesus that I make mine and pass on. The best inheritance I can give my children and grandchildren is the knowledge of God. In the face of what is coming, this has become one of my greatest priorities. With great trust and confidence, I rely on the leadership of Christ. May I be able to respond wholeheartedly, without fear or hesitation, to whatever He does.

I do not want to model myself after the world around me, appealing as it may seem. As Jesus noted, love will grow cold in the days to come, and whole nations will rage against heaven:

> At that time many will fall away and will betray one another and hate one another. Many false prophets will arise and will mislead many. Because lawlessness is increased, most people's love will grow cold. But the one who endures to the end, he will be saved.
>
> Matthew 24:10–13 NASB

> Why do the nations rage, and the people plot a vain thing? The kings of the earth set themselves, and the rulers take counsel together, against the Lord and against His Anointed.
>
> Psalm 2:1–2

This book is an examination of the rage of the nations toward the Church, God's plan to produce a mature Bride at the end of the age, and our righteous response—to grow in an unshakable love for Jesus. It is about believing God and responding to Him in tender love and friendship, drawing near to Him to strengthen our hearts and trouble-proof our lives. But please note, trouble-proof does not mean trouble-free; it means cultivating obedient hearts that take their direction from the rightful Ruler of all nations.

Our present culture does not believe that this matters. People take things into their own hands, driven by their own perspectives and opinions rather than the Word of God. I contend that we must learn to look far beyond self-serving economic concerns or human efforts to bring justice to the earth. We must also adopt a sober mind-set that befits the intensity of what lies ahead.

My hope is that this book is a beginning of a conversation about what you and I are going to do today about what is coming tomorrow.

Maranatha! Lord Jesus, come!

PART ONE

THE CHURCH
AND THE COMING
STORM OF GLORY

1

Preparing to Engage
in the Future Now

Three things are coming in the days ahead: great glory through the Church, great crisis and shaking in the nations, and great judgment from heaven to remove everything that rages against the love and mercy of Jesus. I believe that the Church at large is mostly unprepared for all three of these unfolding spiritual realities.

In this book, I want to examine the current state of affairs in our culture and society and to connect it to where we as Christians are going in the future. I want to empower Christians to adopt a lifestyle of spiritual preparation—the preparation of the heart—so that we can stand strong and faithful, fully participating in the plans and purposes of God for His Church. Along the way, I will discuss a very important premise, namely that the more God's glory and activity are expressed through the Church in a geographic region, the greater the trouble and disruption that follows.

When leaders speak about the current state of affairs in the Western world today, I see two predominant viewpoints: a positive view and a negative view. For some, the Church and the nations of the earth are moving toward a bright, hopeful, glorious future, and the task before the faith-filled Church is to step into her full potential and engage (perhaps even conquer) various spheres and areas of society for the Gospel. For others, these are very difficult and dangerous times, filled with injustice and oppression, and with moral, spiritual and cultural decline. These people believe that the doctrinally sound Church must defend the truth, expose deception and preserve what God has established in our nation, and that the compassionate Church must forsake the old church cultures and structures in order to love the outcast, care for the weak and oppressed, and speak as modern voices for biblical justice.

Christians young and old gravitate toward the kind of church that seems to reflect who they want to be and how they want to engage the world. In many cases, they find it difficult to find an expression of Christianity that reaches for faith, truth *and* love. How is it possible to stand for the truth of the Word of God, believing Him for a victorious future, *and* to walk in mercy and compassion toward the lost (who tend to distort the truth, exploit the poor or oppress the weak, thereby creating their own version of the future)? To many people, it is unclear what the Church is supposed to be in this hour of history. Is the Church supposed to defend the truth? Is it supposed to love the lost? Is it supposed to reshape society around godly values? It is a complex matter to find answers for.

It is hard to find leaders and preachers who tell the larger story of what is being revealed in our day: that God truly is accomplishing great and marvelous things around the nations of the earth, and that there are evidences of His grace and power that are quite unique in Church history. At the same time, the state of world affairs is inarguably growing darker and more anti-Christian. This growing anger against and the rejection of the Church and Christians should cause us to be sober and to reach for fresh deposits of grace, power and courage from the Spirit. We must understand the *whole* story—the positive *and* the negative dimensions of it—in order to have confidence in the leadership of Jesus regardless of our circumstances and pressures. To only hear half of the story of what is currently occurring around the world—of how great things are, or how terrible they are—is to be set up either for great disillusionment or great despair. Only when we are clear on where the Bible says the world is going and what the Church must do about it can we engage with great faith, vibrant truth and passionate love for Jesus and others and be dynamically prepared for the future.

We who are the Church must lean in together in order to hear more clearly what the Spirit is saying. However, it is likely that there has never been a more difficult era in history in which to hear. The noise and traffic within our souls, the many voices in loud disagreement, the many agendas fueled by lust for power and influence—all work against the ability of the saint in the modern world to quiet his or her soul and listen to the clear and beautiful whispers of the Spirit and the Word. Hearing Him clearly is key. How else can we prepare for the great glory and crisis that lie ahead?

The forces at work in modern culture serve to dull the heart and deceive the mind, distracting the Church from the things that really matter. This satanic strategy disconnects the Church from the source of her hope and strength, leaving a people unable to respond to what the Spirit is saying now, unprepared to stand firm in the face of what is coming against the Church in the days ahead. The consequence, according to Jesus in Matthew 24 and Luke 21, is either great deception or deep despair, or both. However, we do not need to be afraid. Rather, we need to be resolved to find the way of wisdom and the grace of God that are available to us. Then we can confidently pursue His heart and perspective for this hour of history.

As we take on an uncertain future, one of the prayers of Paul helps us set the course for understanding, confidence and steadfast love:

> And this I pray, that your love may abound still more and more in knowledge and all discernment, that you may approve the things that are excellent, that you may be sincere and without offense till the day of Christ, being filled with the fruits of righteousness which are by Jesus Christ, to the glory and praise of God.
>
> Philippians 1:9–11

Our aim in this hour of history, which is therefore the aim of this book, is to abound in love with knowledge and discernment, so that we can focus with diligence and courage on the things that matter to God. In doing so, we aim to be sincere (purehearted) and without any offense (toward God or others, even our enemies) until we see Him at His return. The goal of the Gospel is to love Jesus fully. Our growth in knowledge and discernment according to love means that we prioritize the things that produce more love in our hearts for Him over the years. We "approve the things that are excellent" by staying with the things that are fruitful in loving Jesus as well as rejecting or repenting of the behaviors and mind-sets that work against maturing our hearts in love.

Politics, Power and Prophetic Witness

One of the greatest issues facing the Church today is the manner in which we as a people are guided more by ideologies and emotions than we are by theology and devotion. Both liberal and conservative ideologies create narratives about who should or should not lead us and what laws should or should not govern us. People gravitate toward and argue about each side, using fear as a powerful tool to motivate allegiance in order to acquire and keep power. Why do people do this? I believe that it comes from a great lack of intimacy with Jesus, coupled with a shallow understanding of the Scriptures. These deficiencies press Christians to settle for political and ideological substitutes as they seek control over their quality of life.

Or we could say it like this: Christians in the West struggle with varying degrees of feeling powerless, and therefore wrestle with varying degrees of anger within the present context and fear related to the unknown future. This causes many Christians in the modern Western world to see politics and human government as the true power base for sweeping societal changes or the means of their cultural deliverance. They do not see how God endues power to His saints through prayer, by which Christians bypass the powers of this world to connect to the singular Power who reigns over the world. They do not appreciate the way God can invade with His power through His Church to influence a broken world in need of healing and restoration.

Christians are meant to walk in freedom and grace, empowered to live a life of the highest quality. Difficult circumstances, oppressive rulers, wicked laws, opportunistic merchants and systemic sin have very little impact on the Christian who possesses a free heart bound to another King and His glorious Kingdom. As citizens of a heavenly country, we have been appointed to be ambassadors and representatives of our King, witnesses of His beauty and perfect leadership. We are meant to proclaim the goodness and superiority of His love and leadership as it bears much fruit in our interior lives. We are meant to lay hold of something glorious and beautiful on the inside that the world cannot touch, sully or steal; we are meant to display that beautiful holiness to the world around us and draw all men to our righteous King.

We do not, therefore, want to be partisan. We want to be *prophetic*. To be prophetic in the age of wicked, corrupt and oppressive power is to refuse to choose sides. Rather, we long to reconcile the various societal factions to the cross of Christ and call them all to reckon with His controversial, unyielding mercy and justice.

This does not mean that the Church is to be apolitical or politically agnostic. Quite the contrary, the Church is by nature a political entity, part of a heavenly Kingdom under the rule of a Jewish King. The Church and its members express political viewpoints and strong desires regarding the kinds of laws we want to be governed by. Yet the Church is not solely Republican, Democratic, conservative or progressive. The Church is biblical, loyal to the Word of God, subject to the leadership of her King. Therefore our politics must reflect His words, His laws, His heart and His ethics. Our politics are connected to biblical promises that we set our hearts on and reach for in prayer. We labor to advance His Kingdom through good works and the power of the Holy Spirit.

Christians, therefore, seek a *very* political end: the full establishment and expression of the Kingdom of God on earth, in every nation, including and empowering every people group and language. We are not seeking a conservative end, nor are we pursuing a liberal-progressive end. Our desire is for Jesus'

Kingdom to come and His will to be done here on earth in the same manner as His will is expressed in heaven (see Matthew 6:10). Therefore the essence of the "spirit of prophecy" that John spoke of in Revelation 19:10 is to call all sides, peoples and nations to repentance and submission to the love and leadership of Jesus, while bearing witness to His goodness and glory.

We know this to be true, yet the uncertainty and angst related to the pressures and problems of the hour often cause us to drift off course. We want to be connected to the presence, person and power of Jesus, but we often find ourselves adrift and frustrated, wondering what is happening in the world around us and why. Ideological answers from political parties that partially align with our values and views bring a semblance of comfort. We are partially satisfied with and draw a measure of strength from the fact that there are many people out there who agree with us.

Yet our way forward is not found in agreement with others, but in the measure by which we can repent and humble ourselves to agree with Jesus and His Word. As Paul stated, "There is none righteous, no, not one" (Romans 3:10). The journey from insecurity, fear and distress to enduring confidence in the love and leadership of Jesus that stabilizes our lives and secures our future begins with a simple acknowledgement: Only One is fully right in every way, possessing all truth. Everyone else falls far short of the perfect rightness of His ways. Within God and His Word alone can the whole truth be found—as well as the whole unfolding story.

Finding Answers in the Storm

I have spent time over the years with college students, parents and leaders discussing current events and issues of the day. I have found that many of them are perplexed and frustrated, searching for something. With an angst-driven, growing anger at the strangeness of all that is happening in the world today, they are searching for answers. What is happening? Why is it happening? What does it all mean? The noise on the internet, our televisions and our phones barrages us with a continuous chorus of rage, fear, opinions and "answers" from every side. Such answers carry a seductive, seemingly gratifying element in their immediacy. They come in the form of the quick statement, a "gotcha" in which the foolishness and hypocrisy of opposing arguments are exposed, although at times by means of merely shouting over others. By servicing our need for the immediate, cathartic or gratifying answer, loud and brash voices who say what people want to hear gain outrageously large followings, and they gain them very quickly.

Some within the Church have picked up on this, using various means and methodologies. There is a science to marketing and building a following that is quite easy to learn and put into practice. Thus, Christian leaders have learned how to come in either just ahead or immediately behind the issue of the moment. They now emulate the secular voices that have built ideological and philosophical tribes that follow their every word and use their answers as ammunition to win the latest cultural argument. They watch and learn and copy. Now they, too, have answers. In a manner that seems to have emerged through both a slow build and a sudden shift, philosophical tribes have formed along political and ideological lines that all give variations of the same answer, tailor-made to the group that is listening to them. From within the Church and outside of her, the daily news feed of answers, clever insights and trite feel-good proverbs fills the air and clutters our weary souls.

The problem is, today's answers may seem to immediately satisfy the soul in turmoil, but they never provide ultimate satisfaction. The immediate relief that they seem to bring does not solve any particular problem or possess any kind of permanence. Paradigms are not shifted, hearts are not settled and there is very little actual growth or progress as result. The clever answers of the experts, personalities and voices do little but prompt knowing nods, although they may spark a new outrage, even at times inspiring a temporary crusade that seems of central importance today but is quickly forgotten tomorrow.

What is the better way? The Scriptures deem it more valuable than gold and tell us that, when acquired, it has more power and potency than a mere summary statement could ever bring to the human heart. This is the way of wisdom, which Solomon advertised to us so well in the second chapter of the book of Proverbs: Answers are fleeting, but wisdom is a rock of stability that will preserve us, keep us and deliver us from the way of evil (see Proverbs 2:10–12). We need *wisdom*. Wisdom from God is our scarcest and most-needed resource today.

The Slow and Steady Way to Conquer the Future

The very reason you might have picked up this book is that you might be looking for true answers in a world filled with unsatisfactory or insufficient ones. I am hoping that this book serves as a smaller piece of a much larger journey that does not involve sound bites, trite sayings or ideological arguments. I want to replace these with the wisdom of the Word of God as it relates to our current societal context. In the wisdom of God, we can find what we need as we prepare our hearts, lives and families for the future.

There is, however, a great problem associated with the acquisition of wisdom. It does not come easily, nor does it come quickly. According to Solomon, wisdom, so crucial for the preservation of our hearts and lives, is very costly to take hold of. We must work to attain it. We must incline our ears and apply our hearts to the pursuit of wisdom and understanding while simultaneously crying out and lifting up our voices to the Lord (see Proverbs 2:2–3). The apostle Paul spoke of this in relationship to what he called the "spirit of wisdom and revelation in the knowledge of Him" (Ephesians 1:17). Paul prayed fervently and continuously for this work of the Holy Spirit's grace in the lives of the believers of his day. Wisdom is the reward, and there will be great blessing in the life of the one who pursues a deeper understanding of God, His ways and His heart.

Over the years, I have learned about the glorious divine logic behind the time it takes and the cost we must pay to acquire wisdom from heaven. The answers that come from the world around us are so cheaply attained that we value them little and ponder them even less. They may bless us in the moment but do not ever really touch or change our hearts. They have little or no power to form our understanding or convict us into a fresh turning to the Lord. Easy answers usually confirm what we already know or give language to what we already believe. To put it more negatively, they can give us false courage to maintain a very wrong way of thinking. To use Pauline language, they satisfy our "itching ears" with pleasing sounds that mean nothing in regard to our eternal calling in God (2 Timothy 4:3–4).

Wisdom is different. It is meant to reshape our understanding and perspective. Wisdom is meant to strengthen and tenderize our weak, dull, distracted and disconnected hearts by showing us a better way of thinking and doing, while also gently but firmly pointing out our wrong thinking, lack of perspective and unhelpful behaviors. It is not easy. We become comfortable over time with our thinking and behavior, and we remain unaware of how unhelpful our patterns may be in our day-to-day lives. The slowness of the process of pursuing and acquiring wisdom has been established by the kindness of God as the best way of helping us to acquire the kind of understanding that changes minds and hearts. Wisdom that has been built into us slowly and steadily has permanence, and it bears lasting fruit in our lives.

There is a strong prayer component in the acquisition of wisdom; we see it both in Solomon's appeal and in Paul's great apostolic prayer. This serves to remind us that the ultimate source of wisdom is our gracious and merciful God. Wisdom is not something we can earn, although we must make a resolute effort in this costly pursuit.

I have found that the great temptation before every man and woman is the temptation to acquire wisdom through reading the "right" books and engaging with our preferred teachers and preachers. In other words, we are tempted to acquire wisdom as quickly as possible through the same means that we pursue answers. Therefore God withholds wisdom until we seek it out through Him and Him alone, reaching out continually in prayer and even fasting, waiting for Him to supply wisdom to our minds and hearts. He will never be known and understood in the cheap, easy, fast-paced way in which modern people engage with the world around them. He will not give us the extravagantly rich gift of wisdom "on the run," but only over a long period of time in the context of an intimate relationship with Him.

Then, as we see its impact in our lives, we come to value wisdom and, as result, seek God and ask Him for more.

For this reason, the aim of this book is to serve you by grounding your heart and mind in perspectives and biblical ideas that will leave you, over time and after much prayer and conversation with the Lord, positioned to grow in understanding and personal preparation for the days we now live in. This book is not the last word on the subjects presented but merely the start of a long, loving and persistent conversation with the Lord about them.

Anyone can write about and give answers for the current state of the world, and many, many current works already serve this purpose. My aim is the acquisition and the application of the wisdom of Christ.

Preparation for the Return of Jesus

It is not common to hear about how the Church is supposed to prepare for the return of Jesus. Far more common is the idea that His return is something that merely happens to us and to the earth. We must, as that line of reasoning goes, live our lives as normal, godly, responsible Christians until everything suddenly happens. Then, in a moment, everything will be gloriously different around the world.

Jesus, in the gospels, spoke of a more active stance on the matter of His coming; He talked about watching, praying and enduring (see Luke 21:34–36). Apostle Paul used similar language to call believers to prepare for the coming day of the Lord through sober watchfulness and maintaining a right mind-set (1 Thessalonians 5:1–10). Our ultimate goal as Christians who are seeking to engage the future wisely is to grow in our ability to love God well. It will not be easy. Jesus warned us that our love will grow cold. Loyalty to truth, confident faith and hope for the future are all very important. However, love is the greatest, and therefore our highest, priority in this life.

I believe that the Church has a great, glorious and victorious future ahead of her. Proper teaching on the end of the age and the return of Jesus should not produce fear in us. Instead, it should produce hope, awestruck wonder and confidence in the leadership of Jesus and the beauty of His end-time Bride. The certainty of our victory should be saturated with an unsentimental seriousness devoid of human positivism, which chooses to ignore or minimize the negative dimensions of the days ahead. To prepare for the return of Jesus includes a measure of preparation for enduring what is coming, which speaks to steadfast faithfulness and a steady, unoffended heart. We Christians endure the storms of life and the shaking of our world through our diligent pursuit of the life of God that flows within us, striving to abide in the deepest places of true joy found within the heart of Jesus. We lay hold of Him in order to build an unshakable life rooted in His love.

The other reason that we need to study and understand this subject—through prayer, fasting and persistence—is connected to our responsibility and role in helping others to prepare their hearts and lives for the intensity of the days to come. The future will be hopeful, glorious and exceedingly difficult. It is not congruent with a Western paradigm to imagine that something can be both exceedingly difficult and exhilaratingly joyful. However, this is the future that the Bible sets before us: one in which the best days of the Church are ahead (in revival, under the authority of His Holy Spirit, with signs and wonders and many, many salvations), yet one in which some of the most difficult days of global persecution, pain and hardship are ahead for us as well.

The Church will be glorious and powerful at the same time that humanity is unbound in full rebellion against its Maker. In other words, both the Church and fallen humankind will be at the height of their respective powers, whether mature in love for God or full-blown in love for self. During those days before His glorious return, our role is twofold: to help prepare the Church and to turn the hearts of the nations' people to Jesus.

Where the acquisition of wisdom is concerned, not only do we need a proper framework for understanding Scripture, we also need to revive the practice of "pray-reading" the Scriptures as we study them. We do not want to settle only for an understanding of what Scripture means, we want that understanding to inform our prayer life and ongoing dialogue with the Lord. We want to align our hearts with the truth of God's Word, allowing the passages we are reading and praying to stir and awaken us in deeper ways. We want to read a passage, pause, and ask Jesus for greater understanding and clarity. In Ephesians 1:17, this is called the spirit of revelation. We are asking the Spirit to shine His light on the Word of God so that it will become clearer and more beautiful, appealing to our hearts and our minds.

We add to this a spirit of wisdom as we ask the Spirit to give us clear application of the truth. To truly know the Bible is to obey the Bible. How do we walk in loving and loyal obedience to the truth that the Spirit helps us to understand? What does it look like to love Jesus by obeying His commands?

In prayer, as we study God's Word, we make what Jonathan Edwards called sweet resolutions, commitments with tender resolve to follow Jesus in specific ways that, over time, become dear to us. The Word of God is living and active (see Hebrews 4:12). Therefore, we want to continually read, repent and respond to what it says and not develop a habit of passive reading, as if the Bible were merely disconnected stories.

The Bible and truth of God's Word is the Holy Spirit's favorite chariot that He rides upon as He interacts with our lives.

Every time we open our Bibles, we position our lives for a fresh encounter with the Spirit who infuses that Book with dynamic life and grace. To pray and sing the Scriptures is to allow them to reshape our innermost beings. We place ourselves in loving submission to even difficult and challenging truths as often as we are able to talk with Jesus about them.

I want to be haunted by critical passages of Scripture. I want to be disrupted and disturbed by God's truth. The Bible is not merely a therapeutic tool that helps me to find peace or happiness. The Bible is a scalpel in a Surgeon's capable hands, able to cut with absolute precision to the depths of my soul and fashion within me a heart that aches for more of Jesus—if I am willing to allow Him to work.

Position and Prepare Your Heart

How do we position and prepare our hearts for the coming days? This is the central question of this book.

The modern Christian has access to more information about the human condition, human opinions and global events than any other time in history. What does Scripture have to say about these things? This is what I want to examine in this book. I am working with a simple premise: While we have not yet arrived at the destination that the Bible warns about, the trajectory of current trends can easily be connected to that end. This has not always been the case. We find ourselves in the most breathtaking and explosive time in redemptive history, a time unlike any other that has come before. Therefore, we must actively prepare our hearts and lives to engage enthusiastically and joyfully with the leadership of Jesus in the midst of the coming rage and rejection of His leadership by sinful, rebellious people.

Some would disagree with this contention. They cannot align themselves with this framework of relating to the world around us. They argue, "We have been in the end times for thousands of years," or, "Everyone has always believed that they lived in the time of the end." Neither assertion is true.

The first statement, which is based on the idea that the apostles either thought that they were in the time of the end or that the time of the end began in their day, carries degrees of truth without communicating the whole story. The apostles understood that the cross and resurrection of Jesus Christ, the central feature of our Christian faith and the most important moment in all of human history, had set into motion the "time of the end" and the return of Jesus to establish justice, righteousness, peace and the fullness of His Kingdom. However, they also talked about societal, social, moral and spiritual dynamics that would be unique to the future, to a time closer to Jesus' return. They spoke extensively about the unique dynamics and circumstances that accompany the time of the return of Jesus. The time that they (and the prophets) spoke of resembles our era of history far more than theirs.

The second statement, which communicates the idea that the Church has always believed the return of Jesus is near, is factually untrue. We have a very clear record of what the Church believed and taught through every era of church history. We can read the writings of church fathers, detailed documentation of a large number of church councils, personal journals and seminal works that shaped the faith of early Catholic, Orthodox and Protestant believers. These give us much insight into their views on the return of Jesus and their place in that story. In addition, the fact that many within the modern Church concern themselves heavily with the storyline of the return of Jesus and the prophetic Scriptures about it is in itself a sign of the times in which we live.

Such assertions reveal a mind-set that is consciously or unconsciously working to keep these events at a clinical distance from our lives. It is all too easy to treat the prophetic Scriptures like the fables of Camelot, as events of faraway lands that have nothing to do with our everyday lives. It is not difficult to bypass the many Scriptures that emphasize how important prophetic signs are at the end of the age, despite the fact that Jesus taught more than any of the apostles on our need to discern the times, and gave severe rebukes to those who would not pay attention to the prophetic signs that point to His coming.

God promised to give prophetic signs in the generation of the Lord's return as an expression of His mercy, so people can make the necessary preparations for what is coming. Prophetic signs serve the Church in the same way that a weather station signals coming trouble so the people can prepare and be saved. Review what Jesus said:

"Now learn this parable from the fig tree: When its branch has already become tender and puts forth leaves, you know that summer is near. So you also, when you see all these things, know that it is near—at the doors! Assuredly, I say to you, this generation will by no means pass away till all these things take place. Heaven and earth will pass away, but My words will by no means pass away.

"But of that day and hour no one knows, not even the angels of heaven, but My Father only. But as the days of Noah were, so also will the coming of the Son of Man be. For as in the days before the flood, they were eating and drinking, marrying and giving in marriage, until the day that Noah entered the ark, and did not know until the flood came and took them all away, so also will the coming of the Son of Man be. Then two men will be in the field: one will be taken and the other left. Two women will be grinding at the mill: one will be taken and the

41

other left. Watch therefore, for you do not know what hour your Lord is coming. But know this, that if the master of the house had known what hour the thief would come, he would have watched and not allowed his house to be broken into. Therefore you also be ready, for the Son of Man is coming at an hour you do not expect."

Matthew 24:32–44

"Watch therefore, and pray always that you may be counted worthy to escape all these things that will come to pass, and to stand before the Son of Man."

Luke 21:36

See how Jesus commands us to know the generation in which He will return, and how He urges us to pay attention to the signs and indicators that point to His return, watching and praying in response to them.

Taking the commands of Jesus seriously starts a process by which we begin to think about the world around us differently. We begin to think beyond the immediate events that directly impact us as individuals. We begin to see the trends from Scripture progressing around us, toward the appointed end that Scripture describes. We begin to process what Martin Luther King Jr. (quoting an abolitionist named Theodore Parker, who said something similar in 1853) described in 1967 as the "arc of the moral universe" and its course, which he expressed as "bending towards justice."[1]

As we observe and understand the signs of the times we live in, we gain clarity regarding where things presently stand as well as confidence in where things are going. We begin to see the dual strands of history as they have unfolded and will unfold. There is the course that people take regarding their desire to build a world without the God of Israel and His appointed King, our Messiah. The other strand appears mostly outside the notice of mortals in rebellion against God, and it has to do with His leadership of history and His plan for world redemption and restoration.

Both God and sinful humans have a desired end for the course of history and the nations of the earth. To see both ends empowers us to contend in prayer and faith for God's desired end, and to stand firm against the tidal wave of humanity's best attempt to achieve its desired end.

Taking the commands of Jesus seriously helps us to see what we are not necessarily oriented to see as our small, ordinary self-centered lives play out. Unintentionally, we cannot see past ourselves and the small desires of our immediate futures. It is not easy or comfortable for us to detach for a moment and allow our eyes to rise above ourselves so that we can see the bigger picture of what God and the people of the earth are doing.

We tend to procrastinate about undertaking financial discipline, exercise, dieting and other rigorous disciplines. In the same manner, we choose to believe that the return of Jesus has nothing to do with our daily lives and that we do not need to concern ourselves with it. Meanwhile, we have no larger context or framework to help us understand the events that are developing around us, no connection to the broader, global leadership of God upon which to set our hearts with faith and hope. We have very few answers to give those who are seeking them, both from within the Church and from without. We can only evangelize others into our disconnected, self-absorbed agnosticism regarding the events of the end of this age.

We were made for so much more.

The Maker of heaven and earth burns with a deep desire for our partnership and participation in His sovereign plans and purposes. Partnering with God begins with believing God. Our greatest obstacle in preparing for the things to come, in engaging with the plans and purposes of God in our generation, is the fact that we simply do not believe that we need to. We do not believe that we are really at the end of the age and that the return of Jesus is something we need to reckon with.

A soldier will engage in basic training with a different level of intentionality when he actually believes that he is about to go to war. As believers, we are in a real war, right now, and we are confused as to why there are so many more casualties around us than there were a few years ago. The situation around us is intensifying, the cultural narrative against God and His Word is shifting dramatically, the spiritual atmosphere of the earth seems to become more toxic and embracing of an antichrist spirit daily, and yet we engage with our faith in Christ and the power of the Holy Spirit less and less. Our church services are shorter, and our messages are shallower, with less about Jesus and the Bible and more about practical life principles. As a leader in the Body of Christ, I am deeply troubled by the inability of so many believers to stand against the tide of what is happening today, not to mention their unconcern regarding the escalation of evil spiritually, culturally, politically and economically in the days to come.

Positioning our hearts and lives for the days to come means believing that we are in a real spiritual conflict that demands costly choices on our part. We must learn how to genuinely abide in Christ rather than settling for a weekly church service and a life of busyness with little sacrifice and even less true affection for Jesus and His Word. We must recognize that the days are growing darker as people grow in their rage and rejection of God and His Son. Our reasonable conclusion should regard what the Bible says with an awakened and renewed zeal for all that is required of us as believers to thrive and live victoriously in the face of the approaching evil day.

Preparation to Prevail: "The Just Shall Live by Faith"

My final point in the establishment of the trajectory of this book is this: To understand the future and prepare for it spiritually, we must understand what it means to walk in the fullness of what the Lord has made us for. Our future is meant to be one in which we overcome the evil one, triumph over our enemies, walk victoriously and fully in the life and power of the Holy Spirit, and see breathtaking expressions of God's power in the midst of difficult-to-impossible circumstances. Our story is not meant to be about being overcome by the world, struck down by the evil one or losing our way in confusion and disillusionment. As stated earlier, we do not have to be afraid of the future. In fact, the only way for a Christian to become afraid of the future is to be surprised by it and unprepared to face it.

The greatest days of the Church are truly ahead for all of us. The long upward journey of the Bride of Christ over centuries has a glorious apex that will shock the whole world. The destiny of the Bride of Christ worldwide is one of mature love, dedication, beauty and authority as the Spirit finishes His good work in her. The plans of Jesus on a global level are always certain to come to pass. Unlimited grace is available for us to lay hold of as we walk through the dark days ahead, although our future victory depends upon our response as individual believers to the available grace of God.

The prophet Habakkuk and later apostle Paul both declared that "the just shall live by faith" (see Habakkuk 2:4; Romans 1:17). This declaration means that God is going to do what He is going to do, but that we benefit from His sovereign activity and His grace to the measure that we respond by faith. In the face of the oncoming military invasion at the hands of a brutal and wicked foe, God told Habakkuk that his goal was not so much about surviving the onslaught as it was in believing God and moving into an uncertain future with confidence in His leadership.

Paul would adopt this same phrase and idea when speaking to the church of Rome about the Gospel. The good news that has come into our lives is that God, by grace, has made our uncertain futures certain. We can live from a place of security and certainty, which cultivates deep and abiding confidence in God's leadership in our lives despite our own weaknesses and shortcomings. This certainty and confidence—which is part of the power of the Gospel at work in our lives—does not produce passivity (God has done it all; why should I do anything?) but rather a fervent and loyal love. Because we are certain about our ultimate future, we can position ourselves for victory and breakthrough in our immediate future.

This book is not about how to hold on tightly in fear as we wait for the world to self-destruct around us. It is about how the water level of sin and darkness is rising, while simultaneously the water level of the Spirit and His truth increases within the Church.

We can respond with either unbelief or with faith. Unbelief is a conscious choice to lay aside the weapons of our warfare to allow the forces that are driving our world to prevail over the Spirit of God alive within us. Faith is the choice that we make with God's help to face with complete confidence the daunting prospect of our inevitable future. If we believe God's Word and believe that we are in the hour of its unfolding fullness, then faith responds with a confident "yes!" to give ourselves to a lifestyle of leaning into grace. Faith means total trust in His supply of strength and help for the days to come. Faith makes us unafraid of what lies beyond.

The Church and every Christian in it dwell in the "future now." This is the glory and the essence of the Christian faith. To be justified by faith is to enjoy today the benefits and glories of our future verdict before the throne of God. We live free in light of our secured future in Christ, which empowers us to become like Christ. Our future verdict—the resurrection from the dead, a glorified body, an eternity with Christ—gives us boldness and courage to live free and fearless in an age in which many rage against the value system of our heavenly Kingdom.

The Christian engages with the future in a way that is unique to the human race because we have canonized prophecy and the New Testament Gospel, both of which make definitive statements about our future that empower us to position our hearts with clarity and confidence. We can prioritize the things that truly matter. We can give time to the things that are eternal. Our lives and choices have significance and clear continuity with both the immediate future and our ultimate future. The rest of the human race, separated from God, lives only in the moment, for today alone.

As we read this book and others like it, my exhortation is to choose the way of faith, with which you cannot go wrong. The way of faith is the way that brings us into great advantage scripturally. The Holy Spirit's role is to lead us into all truth and tell us of the things to come (see John 16:13), which is why Jesus said that it was to our advantage that He depart:

> "It is to your advantage that I go away; for if I do not go away, the Helper will not come to you; but if I depart, I will send Him

to you. And when He has come, He will convict the world of sin, and of righteousness, and of judgment."

John 16:7–8

It is because of the Spirit and the Word that we are *never* at a disadvantage regarding the future *if we do not want to be.* In an era in which future predictions are common (and often worthless), the Church knows her future, both in this age and in the age to come. And the Church that knows the future can be unafraid today and fully prepared for a victorious tomorrow.

2

Divine Justice and
the Return of Jesus

The Bible speaks about the future by describing what is essentially a drama in three acts. Act 1 involves God confronting the nations of the earth regarding injustice and oppression. Act 2 develops the response of the nations to God's interaction, culminating with act 3—God's response in judgment to the response of the nations. This progression in itself is fairly simple. Our difficulty in comprehending the days ahead of us is not because of some sort of mysterious prophetic symbology or theological complexity. The storyline of redemptive history and its climax is declared repeatedly from within many books and chapters of Scripture, and the details are fairly straightforward in their telling. Our difficulty in comprehending the days ahead as the Bible describes them is related to the unfathomable scope and magnitude of what the prophets declared centuries ago.

In grand language and robust imagery, they described the confrontation between God and the sinful, oppressive, unjust men who hold power and dominion over the nations. They wrote about how the Father desires to repossess the entirety of the earth, breaking the chains of all unrighteous and oppressive rule and freeing His people from a corrupt system of darkness fueled by rebellion against righteousness and godliness. In sweeping prophetic terms, they declared that no corner of the earth will remain untouched or unaffected by His holiness. At the end of the age, everything will be saturated with His incomparable love and glory. This is beautiful, but it is too big and too grand for us to grasp.

It is hard for us to imagine what it will be like: The God of heaven and earth, the Holy One of Israel, the God of all creation, will express His power and declare His will on a global scale during one climactic moment of redemptive history in which every man, woman and child on earth will have to reckon with who He is and what He desires to do as He makes His name known to all.

It has been said that Joseph Stalin once noted: "a single death is a tragedy, a million deaths is a statistic."[1] As humans we think and operate according to scale. Our limitations as rational, thinking beings leave us unprepared for events of global scope and significance. The unimaginably great crises of human history are filled, almost repetitively, with stories of men and women assuring one another that war and events of mass destruction and epic loss are almost impossible in their generation.

The years leading up to World War I (sardonically termed "the war to end all wars") are important to look back on and understand. Europeans lived in a world at that time that was, in many ways, surprisingly similar to ours today. The Industrial Revolution had ushered in very rapid changes that had spurred the emergence of new economic and military powers in Europe. These new leaders worked quickly and quietly to secure their new colonial economic power and safeguard their national security. These developments enriched and emboldened old empires and ancient families who had long held power in the region. They frightened other old powers and families, such as the Russian czars, who were uncertain about their ability to keep pace with the rapid advancement of military technology. European powers planned diligently for the future, preparing for every conceivable outcome of enemy actions against them, yet they were completely and utterly unprepared for what happened.

John Keegan, in his book, *The First World War,* stated, "In 1914 . . . war came, out of a cloudless sky, to populations which knew almost nothing of it and had been raised to doubt that it could ever again trouble their continent." Keegan goes on to say, "Europe in the summer of 1914 enjoyed a peaceful productivity so dependent on international exchange and cooperation that a belief in the impossibility of general war seemed the most conventional of wisdoms."[2] Why is this the pattern of human behavior on the eve of every crisis? How can everyone overlook—and dismiss—the discernable signs and precursors of trouble?

That Great War was impossible for anyone in that day to conceive of beforehand. No one was prepared for modern warfare on a scale of millions of soldiers, and what it would mean for the nations involved, or for the way it would devastate and decimate an entire generation. Their future crashed into their present with sudden and unexpected violence. The ability of men to murder other men with ruthless efficiency on a breathtaking scale was a completely unexpected development. The first two decades of the 1900s brought a perfect storm of progress, new social and political realities, economic and military self-interest and the hubris of powerful men. The modern world collided with the old world, and the nations were not ready for the collision.

To study, even a little bit, the history of World War I is to hear over and over again the phrase, "There had never before been . . ." Historians affix this phrase to everything from the size of the armies, the scope of the battles and the precision of the weaponry to its capability of taking life in entirely new ways and the relentless rate at which tens of thousands would die. Ten million lives were lost, and millions more were powerfully and tragically marked by heartbreak, violence and carnage. The last conflict that had approached this scale had taken place a century prior, during the Napoleonic Wars. No one alive could remember what war of that kind was like, nor could they conceive of or predict the atrocities and pain that would lie ahead of them. Men on horseback who had never faced soldiers with machine guns were slaughtered, and thousands died pointlessly in the bloody fields of the western front.

Two decades after "the war to end all wars," the unthinkable exploded across the world yet again. Mass chaos and warfare exacted a toll on civilization that far exceeded that of the Great War, impossible as that might seem. Though many who were alive during World War II were able to remember the carnage and destruction of the previous war, it was still impossible to predict or conceive of the intensity of the conflict, the unspeakable horrors of human cruelty, or the courage it would take to overcome impossible situations.

My intention here is not to frighten or shock or to be sensational, but I do want to counter one of the greatest dangers we have yet to face in our own generation. It is not war or death or devastation. Rather, it is the sluggish, sleepy complacency that sets in when we yield to disconnected self-absorption, having determined that the lessons of the past have no relevance or bearing on the present or future. Progress and comfort combine together to weave the seductive lie that tomorrow will only be better than today. This is not unlike what occurred in the late nineteenth and early twentieth centuries, when the proud, patriotic, nationalistic citizens of what were then new European economic and military powers read books like Norman Angell's *The Great Illusion,* which told them that the economic self-interest of colonial powers made the prospects of future war practically impossible, and that it was in their best economic interests to coexist, not self-destruct.

Yet humans are humans in every context of history, and regardless of their level of technology, progress or learning, they do what they have always done. History apart from God—when human beings take the initiative to do what is in their hearts to do—continually proves to be an endless cycle of lust for power, warring to gain more power and to keep it, and resisting or suppressing any threats against ever-tenuous positions. One of the great errors of the Western Church that compounds the great danger of sluggishness is the manner in which we, in the name of hope, optimism and positivity, pretend that people today are no longer what people have always been.

In the name of progress and happiness and the bolstering of courage, we tell ourselves that the deplorable things that have happened in the past will never happen again—or if they do, they will happen in faraway places that will not matter as much. (Of course, even right now people are doing the things that they have always done in other parts of the world that are far away from our own. We imagine that progress, economic advancement, technology and modern education have delivered us—the fortunate ones—from the cycles of the past. This is our disconnected naïveté, which can distort our perception.)

This describes how some elements of the Western Church think; it does not describe the whole. Other segments of the Church in the Western world are acutely aware of the injustices and oppression that riddle current systems and arenas of governance. The question for this group then becomes "What breaks the cycle of injustice?" They expect the Church to have clear and helpful answers to the questions of injustice and oppression, sin and growing darkness, and what the future holds.

The simple answer that this group does not seem to recognize is that the answer is Jesus. He is the Man the Scriptures declare as the One appointed by His Father to break the cycle of injustice. It has to be Him, because of the comprehensive scope and severity of our problems, which arise from the depth and complexity of sin on an ancient and global scale.

Jesus and the Justice of God

It is difficult for us to contextualize or understand the intensity of what is to come without understanding the subject of justice. When we understand the dramatic gap between where the world is and where Jesus wants it to be, and when we begin to comprehend the depth of the current injustice and degree of wicked oppression in light of the glory of Jesus' leadership, we begin to align our hearts with His. We can adopt His mind and heart and participate with Him in the necessary processes that will transition this world to the world as it was always meant to be.

For the purposes of this discussion, my simple definition of *justice* is "making wrong things right." The Hebrew word for justice, *mishpat*, speaks of the scope of what is made right; the goal of *mishpat* is the restoration of righteous social order as well as legal equity.

Anyone concerned with justice of any sort must ask key questions: What exactly is wrong? What exactly can be done to set things right? Those of us who believe know that the Father alone is the definer and source of what is right (and, by contrast, the definer of what is wrong). God alone possesses the fullness of clarity regarding what is wrong and the precision of judgment regarding what needs to change. Only He is also filled with mercy and kindness regarding how He brings about the needed changes. Therefore, our great and sole hope lies in allowing justice and judgment to come by means of His leadership and initiative. All other efforts will fall short.

We can understand the patient and merciful manner in which God executes justice in a broken and sinful world if we take a look at how He has worked in our own lives. First, Jesus makes us right within our innermost beings. This begins the process of transforming our thoughts and desires to reflect what is right (what was originally intended for us as created beings).

Gradually, as we walk more and more closely with Him through the events of our lives, we begin to reflect His rightness to the world around us. The Great Commission is the ultimate expression of this principle, being Jesus' great call to the Church to disciple all nations. This is a transformational mandate. The Church makes disciples and works to establish justice in every sphere of society.

The utopian dream of a world set right and filled with justice and blessing has been built into the human spirit since the garden paradise of Eden. Yet it cannot be reestablished all at once. God starts small and works slowly over time, saturating each step of the way with His mercy and kindness. Justice in the hands of any power less than our God, who has the precision of a master surgeon, would be a messy, terrible, violent process. The gap between what is and what should be is vast.

Removing what is wrong and establishing what is right takes time and care, even lifetimes. All the same, we anticipate that the final stages of His plan will be intense and disruptive beyond anything we can imagine.

The prophet Isaiah prophesied about justice more than any other prophetic voice in Scripture. In Isaiah 42, the prophet gave his premier prophecy on the way in which worldwide justice will triumph under Jesus' leadership. Jesus' ministry can be understood in a profound way in the context of this prophecy:

> "Behold! My Servant whom I uphold, My Elect One in whom My soul delights! I have put My Spirit upon Him; He will bring forth justice to the Gentiles. He will not cry out, nor raise His voice, nor cause His voice to be heard in the street. A bruised reed He will not break, and smoking flax He will not quench; He will bring forth justice for truth. He will not fail nor be discouraged, till He has established justice in the earth; and the coastlands shall wait for His law."
>
> Isaiah 42:1–4

This passage provides the clearest biblical model for what it looks like for the Church to engage with Jesus' mandate to establish justice in all the nations. In this same chapter, Isaiah goes on to flesh out God's approach to justice, as follows:

- Justice must be in deep allegiance to Jesus (see verse 8).
- It must be released by intercessory worship (see verse 12).
- It must operate in the Spirit's power (see verses 1, 7).
- It will result in evangelism (see verse 17).
- It will also result in support for the remnant of Israel (see verses 21–22).

- It will energize the lives of the righteous through intimacy with God (see verses 1, 6).
- It will have a forerunner mind-set and lifestyle (verses 16–25).

What is the "forerunner spirit"? In brief, it is the manner by which God gives grace to His people to prepare to fully engage in His plans and purpose in the days to come. This is the underlying theme that we are exploring and developing. Understanding the future from the perspective of the Word of God and preparing for that future by the grace of God as we engage with the wisdom of God, together represent the heart of the "forerunner spirit."

Therefore, in an era of increasing injustice and wickedness, in which we often feel more and more powerless, it is essential to focus on justice and approach it in the way the Scripture teaches us to do. In His parables of the Kingdom found in Matthew 13, Jesus taught that the nature of the Kingdom in this age was to start as a seed, and that the seeds grow in relationship to their environment. Seeds sprout more slowly in darkness. Therefore, what may look small to us today has been growing by the grace of God over much time. Mercy is working slowly, even though our pain causes us to long for more rapid change. God is not willing to pay the price of too-rapid change, if the Church is not yet ready for those changes. Thus, God takes His time, working with faithful urgency, displaying infinite care and faithfulness.

In the process, darkness actually keeps on growing alongside a growing and advancing Kingdom. Everything is moving toward a climactic confrontation between shameless wickedness and a mature Church with her returning King. Inevitably, both the Church and the lost and hurting world display mixed responses. Both the Church and the world are growing in the midst of brokenness, at times responding to the love and mercy of Jesus, and at other times raging against Him.

While the primary subject at hand is the justice of God that will be fully released in the context of the return of Jesus, it is important to note the manner in which the justice of the Kingdom of God expands like a mustard seed, growing since the time of the cross. Jesus released justice partially at His first coming, caused it to increase throughout history, and it will fully triumph after His return, during the age to come.

There is significant continuity of our labors now with what Jesus will do in the age to come. Justice will be released over time with different measures of victory in different geographic areas and in different spheres of society. We, as a people, still long for the fullness of what God wants to bring to the earth, at every phase and in every place.

It is clear that the release of justice must involve both political processes and practical works. Jesus added in Luke 18 that it would also require continuous prayer, night and day, to deal with injustice. Why? While political processes and practical works are a critical component to righting societal and legal wrongs, they do not address the totality of the issue of injustice, which also involves the spiritual aspect of our broken and fallen world. Wrong mind-sets and perspectives, broken thinking, sinful and demonic activity—all contribute significantly to the problems that afflict society and individuals.

The context for this parable on intercession is injustice in the era just prior to the return of Jesus (see Luke 17:22–18:8). Jesus is making a reference to Isaiah 42:1–4, where we see the Messiah releasing justice in the earth. The main thrust of this parable on intercession is for justice in light of the coming cruel and pervasive oppression that is going to trouble every nation of the earth:

Now He was telling them a parable to show that at all times they ought to pray and not to lose heart . . . now, will not God bring about justice for His elect who cry to Him day and night . . . I tell you that He will bring about justice for them quickly. However, when the Son of Man comes, will He find faith on the earth?

Luke 18:1, 7–8 NASB

Jesus spoke of the acceleration of injustice in the days prior to His return, highlighting the need to deal with it holistically, both in the natural and the spiritual realms. He was saying that injustice would not be sufficiently answered by political changes and social action (compassion) because the primary source of injustice is spiritual (demonic). When Jesus asked if He would find faith on earth when He returns, He was asking if He would find agreement that injustice must be addressed with night-and-day prayer. Prayer and the necessary intervention of God speak volumes about our understanding of justice and how it comes about. Will it come through human initiative and human perspective, established like a proverbial house of cards in the strength of man's abilities? Or will it come by powerful divine decree from the Lord into our broken world, which is so desperately in need of His help and correction?

In that light, the answer to the world's problems is simple: Jesus is the Father's answer to injustice.

The Church and the Justice of God

Part of the anger that is boiling and simmering within this generation is the rising sense of how broken the systems are. The economic and political systems of the nations seem to be ideologically barren and bankrupt, the leaders woefully inadequate, and the solutions incapable of bringing satisfactory calm to the growing unrest and unease of the people. Today's explosion of information via the internet only magnifies and expands the amount of knowledge available to the masses, which further communicates how broken the systems are. People with offended hearts want to alert the masses, point a finger and indict the guilty, removing them from the public eye forever. They want to shout, complain, protest, rally and storm the gates of the corrupt powers—to end their reign. Through Isaiah, the Holy Spirit counsels a different way forward.

> "Behold! My Servant whom I uphold, My Elect One in whom My soul delights! I have put My Spirit upon Him; He will bring forth justice to the Gentiles. He will not cry out, nor raise His voice, nor cause His voice to be heard in the street. A bruised reed He will not break, And smoking flax He will not quench; He will bring forth justice for truth. He will not fail nor be discouraged, till He has established justice in the earth; and the coastlands shall wait for His law."
>
> Isaiah 42:1–4

"Behold! . . ."
Behold what? Behold Jesus.
Isaiah made four statements that reveal the Father's plan:

1. Jesus is the victorious One who will bring justice to all nations.
2. Jesus is the One through whom the Father works.
3. Jesus is the Anointed One whom the Spirit empowers. It takes supernatural power to execute the Father's plan.
4. Jesus is the elect One in whom the Father delights. This flows from intimacy with God.

The Father has chosen to bring forth and establish justice on the earth through Jesus' leadership. The way that Jesus leads is the manner in which the Father wants justice to be executed. This is what is meant later on (see Revelation 5), when all of heaven declares Jesus to be *worthy*. Jesus, in His magnificent humility, kindness and tenderness, is the only one able to orchestrate and lead such a dramatic transition in human history. Jesus is the only One who can perfectly navigate the tensions of the nations' rage and rebellion against His leadership and their pride, sin and wickedness, while still maintaining His love, mercy and kindness.

The only One who can be trusted to be generous yet unyielding and uncompromising in acting with righteousness is the Man who is slow to anger, rich in love and aching to see all nations come to the knowledge of His Father. He is infinitely kind. He is completely trustworthy because He is never tempted to please others or to merely make people happy. He can be trusted to do what is necessary to establish all that is right so that love and glory can fill the earth. He is the only One who can execute justice righteously, the only One who can manage the great trials and terrible shakings that will terrify the citizens of the earth.

Jesus *is* justice (see John 8:1–11). Therefore, He is the only One whom the Father endorses, upholds and delights in, related to the otherwise impossible task of executing justice righteously and perfectly.

In verses 2–4, quoted above, Isaiah described Jesus' approach to justice at His first coming. He wants us to take careful note of His approach. It is significantly different from the manner in which human beings who seek power or acquire it express their power and execute justice. Unlike the social justice movements of our day, Jesus did not lift His voice in the street seeking a political or military uprising (verse 2). Again, what is astonishing is the manner in which He moves in meekness and humility, in restraint and in lowliness of heart, offering mercy to all who seek Him, all the while able to cause justice to prevail (verse 3).

As long as there is the possibility of a broken reed being restored or there is a spark of life in smoking flax that has not yet been extinguished, Jesus will restrain Himself. He will restrain the hurricane force of His judgments on the earth as long as there is a way for mercy to be received unto repentance. He is so committed to mercy for the weak and the brokenhearted that He will bear with great resistance to His will; He will press forward with great steadfastness and commitment to His desired end (verse 4). In other words, when we see His mercy, we should not for a minute let that cause us to imagine that Jesus has wavered in any way from His ultimate goal of righteousness and justice.

What is astonishing about verse 4 is the proclamation of Jesus' commitment to see the Father's plan through to the end, despite the great delay of human resistance and national rejection. Isaiah emphasizes that He will not fail nor grow discouraged in any way. He wanted us to know about the steadfastness and patience of Christ, which will bolster us in the long delay between the anguish of injustice and liberation from oppression at the hands of the righteous King who has been appointed by the Father to liberate His people.

Continuing through Isaiah 42, we see more of Jesus' stunning perfection as He walks out the tension between justice and mercy. Moreover, we witness something astonishing: The Father speaks to the Son, giving Him great assurance regarding intimate partnership unto victory: "I, the LORD, have called You in righteousness, and will hold Your hand; I will keep You and give You as a covenant to the people, as a light to the Gentiles" (Isaiah 42:6). Righteousness is seen in each stage of the Father's work, in His methods, His motives and His fruit. Jesus embodies all that pertains to the covenant we have with God.

What does this mean for the Church? How are we to move forward in light of the great injustice and oppression that afflicts the weak?

As social justice movements develop—and now many are emerging from within the Church—we must take careful note here of the prophet's exhortations and encouragements. As voices begin to cry out for justice, what should our response be? "Wait on the Lord," Isaiah counsels (Isaiah 40:31). When more injustices occur, what should we do? "Behold," is all the prophet urges.

We watch and listen to the voice of the Lord and only the Lord. That is how we see the glorious beauty of Jesus and how our ears are opened to hear the wisdom of the Spirit for this hour of history. Jesus declares to us, "Walk in meekness and restraint. I have restrained Myself for a long time. Wait, be patient and listen to Me." Isaiah puts words to His whispers. In an age when a few wrong words can end careers and real sin derails men and women, the mercy and restraint of Jesus in the face of human brokenness speaks clearly to our souls.

His restraint and mercy toward us create space for intimacy with Him; we can come near without shame as we are strengthened by His love. He brings us into partnership with Him and along the way He makes us right in our thoughts, emotions and desires. This makes it possible for the Church to come alongside Him and execute justice. We are to execute justice through restraint, quietness and intimacy with Jesus. We are to make disciples and turn hearts to His way of transformation instead of shouting people down for their errors and shaming them in their brokenness.

In this beautiful way, justice advances—until the time comes when Jesus will no longer restrain Himself.

End-Time Worship, Prayer and Proclamation

Isaiah takes a surprising turn in his discourse on justice and the means by which God establishes it on the earth—he declares a "new thing": an end-time movement of worship and, as Jesus would declare later in Luke 18:1–8, a movement of prayer. Look what Isaiah says:

> "Behold . . . new things I declare; before they spring forth I tell you of them." Sing to the LORD a new song, and His praise from the ends of the earth, you who go down to the sea, and all that is in it, you coastlands and you inhabitants of them! Let the wilderness and its cities lift up their voice, the villages that Kedar inhabits. Let the inhabitants of Sela sing; let them shout from the top of the mountains. Let them give glory to the LORD, and declare His praise in the coastlands.
>
> Isaiah 42:9–12

This is one of the most surprising elements of God's just master plan. How does the Lord want the Church to emulate His meekness and restraint as He engages the spiritual dynamics of injustice on the earth? By inviting the Church to enter into global prayer and worship in unity with His "new song" from "the ends of the earth." Isaiah has just showed us how the scope and power of God's glory will be displayed in the midst of crisis, and now the prophet gives us a detailed glimpse into the breathtaking scale of global worship and prayer. We see in one oracle that this global movement of unified worship will reach as far as every distant and difficult place on earth.

In a parallel again to Luke 18:1–8, Isaiah also connects this global movement of unified worship to the coming of the Son of God in glory and in (shockingly) great passion, zeal and fury.

As the oracle unfolds, we see an exquisite, antiphonal dance between the appointed Messiah and the people. This culminates with the opening of the heavens and the descent of the mighty Man of War, who will lay waste to the mountains and hills with great fury and zeal on behalf of His people:

> The LORD shall go forth like a mighty man; He shall stir up His zeal like a man of war. He shall cry out, yes, shout aloud; He shall prevail against His enemies. "I have held My peace a long time, I have been still and restrained Myself. Now I will cry like a woman in labor, I will pant and gasp at once. I will lay waste the mountains and hills, and dry up all their vegetation; I will make the rivers coastlands, I will dry up the pools."
>
> Isaiah 42:13–15

There are two underlying truths in this passage that Scripture develops elsewhere more fully. (We will explore those passages in the following chapters.) First, a global explosion of worship and prayer presupposes a global explosion of the knowledge of God and the beauty of the One He has appointed to bring justice to the earth. Second, this momentum of glory takes place in the midst of historically grave injustice, oppression and tyranny.

This oracle was delivered at a point in history that featured the most oppression, the most injustice and the most sin and wickedness of any generation.[3] Yet the answer of the people of God to the persecution and injustice was to cry out to God in song. Jesus would declare later that the Church will fill the earth with the good news of the coming Kingdom just before He returns (see Matthew 24:14). The prophet Daniel spoke of a people of understanding who would instruct many in the days to come (see Daniel 11:33). This indicates that the Church will be ready for the storms that are going to erupt across the earth, and she will respond with wholehearted love and loyalty to Jesus. This mature response from the Church in the face of the fury of the nations stirs the Messiah as never before. As a result, He cries out to initiate His long-awaited return.

> "The LORD will roar from on high. . . . He will give a shout, as those who tread the grapes, against all the inhabitants of the earth. A noise will come to the ends of the earth—For the LORD has a controversy with the nations; He will plead His case with all flesh. He will give those who are wicked to the sword . . . Behold, disaster shall go forth from nation to nation, and a great whirlwind shall be raised up from the farthest parts of the earth."
>
> Jeremiah 25:30–32

It is logical then, that the last portion of Isaiah's oracle about how the Father is going to bring justice to the earth in fullness ends with a promise of messengers who will prepare the people for what is coming. Isaiah describes great shaking, wrath, judgment and natural cataclysms in association with the coming of the mighty Man of War who has been appointed to bring the fullness of justice to the earth. In the great delay that springs from His great love, He prepares a Bride who will stand with Him in prayer and adoration in the critical hour in which justice will be fully executed.

The quality of the Lord's preparation of His Bride, the Church, for the things to come is unparalleled; just consider the global scope of prayer and worship and the eventual maturity of the Bride at the most critical moment in history. The Scriptures' promises about the worldwide proclamation of the message of the Gospel of the Kingdom and a great harvest of souls for the Kingdom will be fulfilled before the terrible shaking that is to come. The raging nations of the earth will be shocked into silence:

> "They shall be turned back, they shall be greatly ashamed, who trust in carved images, who say to the molded images, 'You are our gods.' Hear, you deaf; and look, you blind, that you may see. Who is blind but My servant, or deaf as My messenger whom I send? Who is blind as he who is perfect, and blind as the LORD's servant? Seeing many things, but you do not observe; opening the ears, but he does not hear. The LORD is well pleased for His righteousness' sake; He will exalt the law [Word]."
>
> Isaiah 42:17–21

3

Three Storms That Will
Change the World

Let's review what we have learned so far. The severe problem of injustice in the world was met by the person of Christ at His first coming. His faithful steadfastness, meekness and pure heart of great mercy for the broken and bruised meant that Jesus was never discouraged in His quest to grow, over a long period of time, a Kingdom populated by a people filled with wonder, gratitude and adoration for His Father. We read in Matthew 13 that He is willing to allow plenty of time for the proverbial wheat to grow, knowing that the weeds would be growing mingled in with it.

Chapter 13 of Matthew's gospel also records many other parables that Jesus told about time and process in His Kingdom. The Kingdom of God, He said, is like a mustard seed that starts out almost imperceptibly small, inevitably growing into the greatest tree of all. He added that the Kingdom is like leaven, the hidden agent within bread that causes it to rise and grow into its full expression. The parables also include descriptions of the negative side of the process, such as the angelic host casting out the things that offend God and throwing into the furnace of fire those who practice lawlessness. Despite God's supreme patience, we see that the wicked will be separated forcibly from the just, who are called "sons of the Kingdom."

Then we read Isaiah's description of how the Kingdom will expand until it reaches every faraway place on earth where people can be found who are like the King in His meekness, humility, lowliness of heart, mercy and tenderness—people who worship God with great abandonment in the face of historic injustice.

The final act of the drama is the second coming of Jesus to the earth. He will vindicate His people, separate the wheat from the tares, and establish full justice and righteousness in Jerusalem and around the world. Yes, God is patient, slow to anger and rich in mercy and loving-kindness. But He will reach the end of His considerable forbearance. There is a line of demarcation regarding injustice and oppression.

As the Kingdom comes into fullness and maturity around the world, so too will sin, wickedness and darkness. Sin will fully bloom into a seductive, corrupt, deceitful expression of power and human potential that will ensnare millions around the world.[1] The issue that the Bible confronts us with regarding the maturity and fullness of wickedness, unrighteousness, injustice and oppression at the end of the age is not about individuals themselves engaging in darker acts of sin—though there is an element of that.[2] This development of sin and darkness involves the normalization, legitimization and systemization of sin as it relates to the world that sinful men will build and the ideas that they will build around. We will look at this with much more in-depth when we examine the birth of the cultural narrative that currently fuels much of the anti-Christian thought around the Western world.

These complex systems of sin have been built over centuries to uphold and support economic and political systems that enable the acquisition of much wealth and power for the few at the expense of the many. The particulars of the ideological systems are irrelevant and interchangeable. In all of these systems, broken, sinful men operate in varying degrees of stubbornness, pride, presumption, ungodliness and unrighteousness. Hence, in a fallen world, Paul's commentary on the psalms about the human condition stands truer than ever: "There is none righteous, no, not one" (Romans 3:10; see also Psalm 14:3). In other words, at its best this world is being led and governed by sincere but misguided people; at its worst, this world is being exploited by truly wicked and evil people who leverage their power in order to gain more and keep it.

The end result of human corruption is that the world systems have been built on vain imaginations and empty philosophies—in other words, world systems are nothing but houses of flimsy cards. Wicked people and their governments create more problems long-term than they can solve, and over time, all of the cracks and problems expand and multiply.

Apart from the loving intervention of God, there is no end to the injustice and exploitation of the weak. That is the underlying reality for the magnitude of what is to come: God Himself will step into the affairs of men, moving in unprecedented power to uproot deeply ingrained systems of wickedness and transitioning the world into the age to come. God's highest desire is the restoration of all things, by which He makes all things new.

These are monumental events of immeasurable significance, the most critical and world-defining moments in all of redemptive history. Therefore, the Bible describes a sequence of escalating events that culminate with Jesus breaking through the sky to return to the earth, specifically to Jerusalem.

To the measure by which He inserts Himself into our world at that time is the measure with which powerful, wicked men will rage in their response. When God comes, He will come as the God of light and truth. His light exposes the deeds of darkness, and it allows us to see the truth of humanity apart from God, ending our petty arguments and debates. Things will become very, very clear when God steps onto the global stage, and no one who knows and loves Him will argue with what the light of His glory reveals. In fact, no one will argue with His righteous judgments at all when everything is revealed and the Church is vindicated before the entire world.

At the end of the age, the Church will love the judgments of the Lord (see Revelation 16). The nations will rage against them, but no one will have an argument to make against the righteous sovereignty of the Father.

Prior to Jesus' return, three "storms" will envelop every nation and every person on earth. The end result of these three storms will be a different world—one that is renewed, transformed and filled with the unrestrained glory of the Lord. In this chapter, I will introduce the three storms that are coming in those days, before examining them in more detail in later chapters.

The First Storm: Revival and Outpouring of the Spirit

The difficulty with using the word, *revival* to discuss the future and what lies ahead for the Church and the nations is the way in which that term is understood by various groups and denominations today. For some churches, *revival* indicates a meeting

72

or series of meetings designed to invite the activity of the Holy Spirit. For other ministries, the word *revival* represents an ever-present reality of a growing, victorious Church. They would say that to see megachurches growing, mission endeavors thriving, and a spark of Holy Spirit power on individuals and ministries signifies that we are experiencing a measure of revival now. For others, revival is something to contend for in prayer, wait for in expectation and predict in prophetic utterances. For those who are skeptical of it, *revival* is shorthand for emotionalism, hype and destructive manipulation.

As Arthur Wallis once wrote in his book, *The Day of Thy Power:* "There was never a day in which the term 'revival' needed to be more carefully defined."[3] He continued, explaining that

> Revival can never be explained in terms of activity, organization, meetings, personalities, preachings. These may or may not be involved in the work, but they do not and cannot account for the effects produced. Revival is essentially a manifestation of God; it has the stamp of Deity upon it which even the unregenerate and uninitiated are quick to recognize. Revival must of necessity make an impact upon the community, and this is one means by which we may distinguish it from the more usual operations of the Holy Spirit.[4]

While I love prophetic proclamations of coming revival that fit Wallis's definition, I am not in the position to make any predictions of my own. My interest is in Wallis's definition of revival as it is applied to a biblical promise of what is to come prior to the return of Jesus. For the modern charismatic or Pentecostal Church, prophecies and promises of future revival are exciting and hopeful, producing a sense of joyful expectation about the days to come. For the prophets of old who proclaimed a global, end-time outpouring of the Holy Spirit, the revival that will presage the coming of the Messiah signified a warning as much as it serves as a promise.

For the prophets, revival was a storm.

It might seem strange to think about revival in this manner. We have learned to focus only on the benefits of revival rather than stepping back to view revival in its full context. Of course it is never wrong to be stirred by the stories of revival, to be encouraged in our faith, to be awakened in our expectation or to long for more of the presence of God. It is, however, naïve to focus solely on the healings, salvations and miracles and to ignore the other side of the story of revival.

Revival brings a sudden introduction of unstoppable power and an unavoidable presence of God to a people who, left to themselves, would have been content to live their lives free from the interference of God. We forget that people, for the most part, want to be left alone and undisturbed. Uninvited disruptions that they do not understand are normally not welcomed and celebrated, even if the end result of that disruption proves to be a positive development.

People naïvely assume that *revival* means "everyone is saved," but historically, this has not been the case. Historically and biblically, *revival* has always meant "everyone decides." Revival happens when God steps into a geographical region with power, like a bright light shining into a dark room, forcing everyone to deal with the fact that God is real. They see who God really is, and they find out what God really cares about. In a smaller-scale revival, this kind of intrusion of God's presence causes a great disruption. On a much larger scale, which the Bible discloses will occur as a future event, the global incursion of God's power will function like an overwhelming storm of glory.

The Second Storm: The Rage of the Nations

Why will the end-time revival disturb the nations so much? The reason it will affect the nations like a storm is that this final outpouring of the Spirit will suddenly set very real power upon the Church in the midst of the nations. The revival will produce a dramatic shift in power, a competing power, and this will present a choice for the multitudes between two worlds that possess opposing value systems, rewards and rules for success. And new power of any sort will always be a threat to another more established power. In this case, the emerging power of a revived Church will present the likelihood of a mass exodus of millions of new converts from corrupt world systems to the Church, as they shift their loyalties and, most importantly, their finances.

In other words, the plan of God in the days to come is to make His Church a power that the nations of the earth must reckon with. This will provoke the secular, governmental powers of the earth to much anger. Their furious reaction may seem to be abrupt, but in fact it will come from the simmering, ancient hatred of and rage against the God of Israel, which has been within the human heart since the Fall in the Garden of Eden. In other words, human rage against God is always flowing beneath the surface, and all it takes is a spark of God's proximity to light the flame of fury. Once ignited, it explodes with the pent-up bitterness of centuries of desire to be free of God and to be rid of His imposition of authority.

Thus, we see that when God sets power upon His global Church, it will ignite a storm of rage from the nations that will be like nothing anyone has ever seen before. In that day, the truth of the human condition apart from God will be laid bare for all to see. God is light, and when He shines, the light of His countenance into the darkness of human rage and rebellion, it will be exposed beyond doubt or argument that all of human civilization wallows in sin and unrighteousness. On a personal level, the light of God's truth will remove all sentimentality and vanity that come from a fallen, carnal perspective regarding sin. Individual men and women will be confronted with the need to be zealous and passionate in their own lives, to repent and humble themselves before the Lord.

This is the core reality of the revival of God and the outpouring of the Holy Spirit, and this is why Scripture tells us about the inevitability of the rage of the nations that will follow. God's glorious arrival onto the sinful human scene is at the same time both merciful and confrontational. He comes for the purpose of showing us the truth—about Himself and about ourselves—so that we might repent, turn from our wickedness and submit our lives to the authority and leadership of Jesus. This is God's great desire—that none should perish, but that all should come to repentance (see 2 Peter 3:9).

The great problem that the apostle Paul called "the mystery of lawlessness" (2 Thessalonians 2:7) is one that we have to reckon with honestly as we deal with the present and future rage of the nations; the fact is that many do not want to repent. Many do not want to turn from their wickedness and do not want to come under the authority and leadership of Jesus. Filled with unadulterated pride and stubbornness, people want to be left to themselves to live life as they desire.

We can see that the root of the rage of the nations is found in the hearts of men and women who agitate restlessly for separation from God, freedom from His moral code and law, and freedom from accountability, driven by a relentless desire for independence to build their own world (different from the one the Bible declares is coming). The future storm of the nations' rage is the explosion of a dying world that refuses to draw its last breaths, the reaction of sinful individuals who want to maintain their unbridled world of sin, doing with it as they please. As Jesus declared, "And this is the condemnation, that the light has come into the world, and men loved darkness rather than light, because their deeds were evil" (John 3:19).

The Third Storm: The Judgments of the Lord

One of the most challenging scriptural subjects for Christians is that of God's judgment on the wicked, powerful oppressors of the earth at the end of the age. The doctrine of the wrath of God is central to all biblical implications, yet the corridors of human history echo with the cry "Unfair!" because of it. Our own hearts echo this. In fact, we could say that this doctrine is the most hated biblical doctrine. (It is equally the most neglected and most misunderstood.) This is tragic because in fact the doctrine of the wrath of God is *crucial* to understanding the bounty of God's love.

Only the actual Word of God can break down the lies that surround the certainty of God's wrath, which is more real than the words on this page.

We cannot understand even a portion of the measure of God's love without a better understanding of the measure of His wrath, which is a dynamic part of His love, passion and jealousy for our good and our wholeness. As with the doctrine of justice, to the measure that we are able to see the great problem will we see God's great solution. To put it into different words: As long as we are dull and insensitive to the blazing wrath of God, we will remain dull and insensitive to our absolute protection from it by the gift of righteousness promised to us in the Gospel. When understood properly, the weight of this doctrine will produce in our hearts a depth of gratitude to God that will vastly increase our love for Him.

There are two distorted views of God's wrath and judgment that we must work through.[5] The first is too *personal*. This view overemphasizes the idea that God's anger is like man's anger, with elements of personal vindictiveness and revenge; His purposes have been crossed so He administers payback. The other distortion renders God's wrath and judgment to be completely *impersonal*. This view rationalizes that the wrath of God is little more than "paying the bill" for wrongdoing; because there is a built-in, passive, moral order in the world, whatever a man sows, that he will also reap. This impersonal moral mechanism is not the same as the biblical wrath of God, and it has led people to believe that God is never angry with any individual.

People have always objected strongly to the idea of God's wrathful judgment. In fact, you could say that humankind *hates* it. As we know too well, we prefer to create gods in our own image so that we can justify our pursuit of pleasures that are outside of God's will. Doing this means that we turn our faces away from the truth, which keeps us from comprehending God's mercy and love. We end up thinking of God as an angry, unreasonable dictator, instead of seeing ourselves as inherently evil and in need of His redemption.

The Scriptures assert that human beings need to be reconciled with their Creator personally, that He has every right to treat our rebellion with wrath, but that He, in His overriding love has, through Jesus, provided a way for us to come clean. This is good news—if we will accept the truth that it is based on. We need to stop hating the concept of God's wrathful judgment and stop buying into the false notion that we are basically good children in conflict with a cranky Father. Such a "gospel" only keeps Christianity man-centered and weak.

This is the root system and foundation for the rage of the nations. When individual hearts rage against the righteous judgments that God levels on wickedness, injustice and oppression, soon whole populations and cultures become enraged against God. The very idea of being held accountable to God for our actions, with the dire consequence of divine wrath, awakens deep and powerful emotions within the human soul. If we Christians, who purposefully seek to love and follow Jesus, tend to distort or ignore altogether this doctrine of the wrath of God, how much more do non-Christians have trouble with it? Worldly and prideful (and often powerful) people prefer to run their own lives without regard for the potential consequences of their sinful actions. Self-assured, they never think about a future day of reckoning in which the accounts of heaven will be settled according to a righteous Judge whom nobody can bribe or influence. There is an already-and-not-yet dimension to God's wrath, just as there is for salvation. His wrath is manifested both in the present and in the future.

By means of the cross of Christ, God points all people to the revelation of His love, mercy and kindness, as well as the revelation about His wrath and judgment against all ungodliness (sinful attitudes about God) and unrighteousness (sinful actions against God). Through the cross God extends His invitation to all: "Come and receive life from Me through repentance. Receive My free gifts of mercy and righteousness. I love you, and I want you to be where I am."

In actuality, how does God extend this invitation? How does He point people to the cross to receive His offer of mercy and renewal? Throughout history, He has accomplished it through the preaching of the Church and the strong power of the Holy Spirit on the gospel message. That is the "already" aspect of His coming Kingdom. Then there is the "not yet" aspect: the future day in which every gospel proclamation of the Church will be filled with unprecedented power through the yet to come outpouring of the Holy Spirit.

In that day, people will receive an amplified invitation to come and drink from the fountains of God's love and mercy. And this amplified invitation will inevitably be associated with amplified consequences for refusing God's invitation, as Paul notes:

> Therefore you are inexcusable, O man, whoever you are who judge, for in whatever you judge another you condemn yourself; for you who judge practice the same things. But we know that the judgment of God is according to truth against those who practice such things. And do you think this, O man, you who judge those practicing such things, and doing the same, that you will escape the judgment of God? Or do you despise the riches of His goodness, forbearance, and longsuffering, not knowing that the goodness of God leads you to repentance? But in accordance with your hardness and your impenitent heart you are treasuring up for yourself wrath in the day of wrath and revelation of the righteous judgment of God, who "will render to each one according to his deeds": eternal life to those who by patient continuance in doing good seek for glory, honor, and immortality; but to those who are self-seeking and do not obey the truth, but obey unrighteousness—indignation and wrath, tribulation and anguish, on every soul of man who does evil, of the Jew first and also of the Greek; but glory, honor, and peace to everyone who works what is good, to the Jew first and also to the Greek. For there is no partiality with God.
>
> For as many as have sinned without law will also perish without law, and as many as have sinned in the law will be judged by the law (for not the hearers of the law are just in the sight of God, but the doers of the law will be justified; for when Gentiles, who do not have the law, by nature do the things in the law, these,

although not having the law, are a law to themselves, who show the work of the law written in their hearts, their conscience also bearing witness, and between themselves their thoughts accusing or else excusing them) in the day when God will judge the secrets of men by Jesus Christ, according to my gospel.

Romans 2:1–16

There is ongoing debate in various parts of the Church today about the judgments of the Lord. One assertion is that God does not judge because He is love. However, the Scriptures give us a completely different picture: Through the Word of God, we see God act in judgment *because* He loves. He loves us and our world far too much to leave it as it is. Therefore, He acts, moves and intervenes within human affairs to remove every hindrance to His love.

The Day of the Lord

One final doctrinal concept to consider as we study the righteous judgments of the Lord is the doctrine of "The day of the Lord," a phrase used nearly a hundred times throughout Scripture. The day of the Lord is presented by the prophets Isaiah, Jeremiah, Joel, Zephaniah, Zechariah and Malachi, then later in the New Testament by Jesus and Paul, as the time in history in which all the nations will be forced to respond to the Lord as He reveals Himself to all in power, majesty and glory.

The day of the Lord is the ultimate storm that the human race will endure prior to the coming of Jesus. Everything will be shaken. As God sets power on His Church to proclaim His Gospel that many might repent and be saved, the nations will rage violently at the pronouncement of coming judgment. And in that hour of history God will act according to the warnings of the prophets of old.

Does this seem unfair or unwarranted? Those who resist the idea of God shaking the nations in accordance with their rage, rejection and rebellion should remember that long before God will come in His great wrath with cataclysmic shaking and judgment, He will have sent out wave after wave of His messengers with the Gospel. Those of us who believe have been numbered among those messengers.

Next, He will have sent revival and a storm of glory to capture the attention of the people, to urge them to repent and receive the free gift of God's love, mercy, righteousness and renewal. By this means, He will have given them every opportunity to understand and believe the truth. Then His time of judgment will arrive, but even in the midst of it, He will offer a way out. He will shake lives, economies and systems progressively over a series of judgments rather than striking the earth in one instantaneous act of annihilation.

When we understand that this series of storms will occur in sequence over a period of time, allowing much time for people to repent and turn from their destructive path, it helps us view God's wrath in a very different light. As stated earlier, it helps us to understand His extravagant love and mercy better when we know that He will give even the worst offenders plenty of time to turn and enter into His kindness and grace.

God will not simply step into history and strike the wicked and the powerful down in anger. In humility, tenderness and great mercy, the God of all creation, the Maker of heaven and earth, will step into history and *plead His case with the nations*.

Who is this, our all-loving God, who is so extravagant in showing His mercy? How much more does it make us want to surrender ourselves to Him?

4

The Coming Storm of Revival

Throughout history, God has consistently chosen to show His greatness and glory by expressing His power in and through weak and broken people like you and me. This is one of the most beautiful aspects of the Lord's sovereign leadership over the earth, and it is the way He chooses to demonstrate His incomparable might and power to the nations of the earth.

By valuing the weak and the foolish things of the world—the small, overlooked, oppressed, powerless and broken—the things that do not make the news or win the prizes in modern society, God turns worldly values on their head. He rewards quiet faithfulness and obedience, and He listens to the heart-felt prayers of those who worship Him. He is not impressed with self-important men, even kings and princes, because the only things that really matter eternally are the things that He establishes.

In writing the book of Ecclesiastes, King Solomon established the most powerful apologetic ever written for the prioritization of what truly matters where our time, energy and passions are concerned. He exposed the folly, vanity and meaninglessness of a life spent in empty pursuits in his often-quoted key line: "I have seen all the works that are done under the sun; and indeed, all is vanity and grasping for the wind" (Ecclesiastes 1:14).

A life spent in the pursuit of pleasure or legacy—even a legacy that appears to be noble—means a lot of stressful, hard work. And to what end? Once you perish, it blows away. "All is vanity." The only labors that are worth undertaking are the ones directed by the one and only true King. These are meaningful because they will last for eternity. Solomon wrote, "I know that whatever God does, it shall be forever. Nothing can be added to it, and nothing taken from it. God does it, that men should fear before Him" (Ecclesiastes 3:14).

When He came to earth, the Son of God became the very wisdom of God. From the accounts in the New Testament, we know many details about His three decades of life that culminated in a dishonorable crucifixion. In the eyes of the world, His accomplishments seemed utterly wasteful and foolish. Yet we who know Him and who follow Him as our beloved Savior and Lord recognize that none of His words have ever fallen to the ground and that His accomplishments are greater than those of anyone in the entire history of civilization. And now here is the Father, summoning the willing disciples of Jesus, we who lovingly and faithfully seek to adopt His values and to go out into the world to advertise the wisdom of Jesus' life, death and resurrection. Jesus' disciples were a disparate assemblage of very weak people. Only a handful of us occupy positions of importance in the world's eyes. The very fact that we are willing to adhere to the Gospel message and to endure suffering with joy exposes the futility of the powerful people who receive the accolades of the world.

Throughout Scripture we read about the desire of God to remove power from those who are unworthy to wield it—unjust oppressors who take advantage of the poor to build their own wealth and comfort—and to give that power to the "saints of the most High" and the "meek and lowly of the earth."[1] The Father's plan from the beginning has been to have a people for Himself that He could present to His Son as an eternal companion.[2] The Bible speaks of the Bride of Christ as consisting of God's redeemed—those who are saved, sanctified and mature in love. This maturity develops over a lifetime of responding in love to His work of grace. Over the years of their lives on earth, individual believers are transformed into the likeness of Christ, and collectively they make up the Church.

This transformation is a lifetime process. From our point of view, it may feel slow and almost invisible. But it is successful. The Father takes shallow, immature, self-centered human beings and changes them into passionate friends of Jesus who will give their lives wholeheartedly to serve Him. These are the ones to whom the Father desires to give a mighty inheritance; they will govern over the earth alongside Jesus, the returning King. Meek and lowly on the earth, they do not see power as an opportunity for personal enrichment but rather as an opportunity to bless and serve others.

The Struggle of Power: Loss and Gain

When Paul spoke of God using the "foolish and the weak things of the world" to shame the strong and the wise, by implication the prideful strong must be put down and deprived of their status and control (see 1 Corinthians 1:27). Unworthy, oppressive overlords must become underlings.

Paul is not speaking only of a future eventuality. Such power struggles often ensue when God moves to take power from one group and give it to another. This was the reason that the Pharisees and Sadducees were so enraged regarding Jesus, particularly as He entered into Jerusalem, the capital city of Israel, at the height of His ministry and notoriety among the people. In one particular confrontation with Jesus, they challenged His authority in front of the people, and Jesus responded with His parable about the absentee landowner whose servants—and finally his own son—were killed one after another by the wicked tenants (see Matthew 21:33–44). And "when the chief priests and the Pharisees heard Jesus' parables, they knew he was talking about them. They looked for a way to arrest him, but they were afraid of the crowd because the people held that he was a prophet" (Matthew 21:45–46 NIV).

The Pharisees did not like what Jesus said, and they understood the implications of the parable, the threat that Jesus represented to their power. Whether or not they believed He was truly who He claimed to be, they were "afraid of the crowd," which showed their comprehension of the facts: Jesus' influence over the masses gave Him power—and it was clear that their own continuation in power was not a feature of His future plans.

This is an element of the storyline behind the crucifixion of Christ that we rarely take into account. For the Jewish religious leaders to arrest Jesus and have Him executed by Rome as a traitor put them at considerable risk. In general, the Jewish leaders that governed the religious affairs of Israel preferred to avoid interactions with Rome, and they lived in terror of the ever-present sword of Roman justice. Therefore, for these Jewish religious leaders to go ahead and appeal to the power and authority of Rome to deal with the threat Jesus represented speaks volumes about their fears of losing their power and authority because of this itinerant rabbi.

The issue that we as the Church need to wrestle with, then, is with the stated desire of our God to take and give power, and what the wicked and unworthy ones who presently possess that power intend to do about it.

Global Outpouring of the Holy Spirit

"And it shall come to pass afterward that I will pour out My Spirit on all flesh; your sons and your daughters shall prophesy, your old men shall dream dreams, your young men shall see visions. And also on My menservants and on My maidservants I will pour out My Spirit in those days. And I will show wonders in the heavens and in the earth: blood and fire and pillars of smoke. The sun shall be turned into darkness, and the moon into blood, before the coming of the great and awesome day of the LORD. And it shall come to pass that whoever calls on the name of the LORD shall be saved. For in Mount Zion and in Jerusalem there shall be deliverance, as the LORD has said, among the remnant whom the LORD calls."

Joel 2:28–32

Joel 2:28–32 contains one of the most powerful promises from God in the Bible. Joel's prophecy states that God will, at the end of the age, pour out His Spirit on all flesh across the earth. Joel describes a global outpouring of the Holy Spirit across the earth, the likes of which we have never seen before, and he prophesies about four significant expressions of the power of God that will happen all at the same time. These four expressions of God's power are to be followed by a breathtaking and terrifying response from the nations and also by an unprecedented explosion of God's blessing upon His people. What are these four expressions of God's power?

As I will go on to explain in the rest of this chapter, they are as follows:

1. Global activation and engagement of the Church
2. Signs and wonders that shake heaven and earth
3. Global salvation for all who respond to the Lord
4. Prayer, missions and revival that awaken and provoke the nations

Throughout church history, starting with the accounts in the book of Acts, revivals have taken place on a local, regional and national scales. In the past couple of centuries, we have seen notable revivals, including the First and Second Great Awakenings, the Welsh revival, Hebrides revival and the Jesus movement. However, we have not yet seen a global revival such as the one Joel prophesied about. The outpouring of the Holy Spirit described by Joel goes far beyond the experiences we have known, as wonderful as they have been. In past revivals, the gift of the indwelling Holy Spirit has been activated in large numbers of people, but Joel is describing an unprecedented worldwide move of God.

Some have understood this passage to be speaking of the outpouring of the Holy Spirit upon the 120 disciples in the Upper Room at Pentecost because of the apostle Peter's use of Joel's prophecy to explain to the crowds what was happening (see Acts 2:1–21). However, it seems more likely that Peter was using the promise of a future global outpouring of the Spirit on all flesh to give context and clarity to a present local outpouring of the Spirit on some flesh. Many details within Joel's prophecy are missing in the Acts 2 outpouring of the Spirit on the early Church.

Joel 2:28–3:21 records one continuous prophecy that speaks of a comprehensive event that has significant global consequences and impact. Perhaps our knowledge of these many preliminary outpourings of the Spirit can help us imagine what it will be like. Take one of the historic revivals that you know most about and think of it multiplied manyfold, to a worldwide level—throughout every nation on every continent, everywhere that people live. Imagine the phenomenal power of the Holy Spirit being poured out across the whole planet in every village, town and metropolis, on isolated farmsteads and in jungles, on board every ship and airplane—simultaneously. What would it look like to have a combination of the day of Pentecost, the First Great Awakening and the Azusa Street revival happening everywhere on earth at the same moment in time?

Global Activation and Engagement of the Church

The first sign that Joel is describing a unique revival is the high level of engagement of the people of God. This will be an all-hands-on-deck activation of God's people, young and old. Every single believer on the earth will be in full agreement with God and in full unity with one another across cultural and denominational lines (see Ephesians 4:13). Joel's use of the phrases "your old men" and "your young men" speaks of the extent of the power of God upon everyday believers. In the time of the prophet Joel, this was unheard of; the power of the Holy Spirit was known to rest upon a certain few men or women for the accomplishment of specific functions or assignments. In any given generation, only one or two individuals might be selected for such an honor. Here, Joel is envisioning a future time in which the people of God will all be anointed with an unusual spirit of prophecy in order to take part, with authority and power, in what God is doing across the earth.

We must note the difference throughout Scripture between "the Holy Spirit *within*" and "the Holy Spirit *upon*." The latter was the Old Testament pattern. As Christians of the New Covenant, we enjoy a dynamic union with God in Christ through the indwelling of the Holy Spirit *within* our innermost being. This profound and glorious new state of being arises from Jesus Christ's free gift of righteousness. It is a powerful and beautiful interior uniting of our spirit with the Spirit of God. Paul spoke of believers in Jesus being "sealed with the Holy Spirit of promise, who is the guarantee of our inheritance until the redemption of the purchased possession" (Ephesians 1:13–14). The indwelling Spirit is both the sign and the seal of the New Covenant of God for those who believe, which gives us great assurance of our eternal destiny with Christ in the days to come and our position in Christ right now. Christ within is our great hope, and we draw much confidence in our day-to-day life from this fact. Having the Holy Spirit within was not the experience of the prophets and others who are portrayed throughout the Old Testament.[3]

According to Joel, in the last days the Lord is going to empower *everyone* who loves Jesus with the power of the Holy Spirit. By filling His people with the power of the Holy Spirit for the working of miracles, healings and more, God intends to capture the attention of the whole world—the self-absorbed, the powerful, the poor, the broken and oppressed, the lost. This is a breathtaking picture of the breadth and scope of the Lord's heart and plan. Our earlier look at Psalm 2 and Matthew 24 also confirms the scale of God's outreach in that day:

All of the kings and rulers of the earth will have heard of the coming of the Lord's anointed King whose inheritance is the nations of the earth—and all nations will hate the Church for the sake of the name of Jesus.

It is stirring and sobering to imagine that time to come. The Church around the world—every saint, every denomination, in every tribe and language—will be unified in its proclamation of the returning King, and the message of His coming will be punctuated with unprecedented power from the Holy Spirit to capture the attention of the people regarding that message. In addition, they must also face fierce and unparalleled opposition.

Signs and Wonders That Shake Heaven and Earth

Beyond the activation and engagement of the saints, Joel also spoke of the extraordinary scope of the power of God that will come upon His people in the days to come. Joel proclaims that supernatural wonders that have never yet been seen in the history of the world will shake the nations and capture the attention of the people.[4] God will empower His people with such a glorious message that the nations will believe and respond to His mercy.

Much later the prophet Haggai made a similar declaration: "For thus says the LORD of hosts: 'Once more (it is a little while) I will shake heaven and earth, the sea and dry land; and I will shake all nations, and they shall come to the Desire of All Nations'" (Haggai 2:6–7). The writer of Hebrews repeated Haggai's prophecy, referring to it as a promise from the Lord to remove the things that could be shaken, "that the things which cannot be shaken may remain" (Hebrews 12:27). The prophets are foretelling a future inbreaking of the power of

God across the earth that is without precedent in history and almost unimaginable in its scope and impact. It is hard for us to imagine a book of Acts revival happening worldwide and not merely in one city or one region. Add to this a book of Exodus level of signs and wonders happening globally and concurrently with this outpouring of the Holy Spirit, and it becomes even more difficult to imagine. The magnitude of what the Bible is describing about the days to come is far too great for our limited minds to grasp.

Yet our limitations will not deter the progress of God's will. He desires the whole of the earth to see His glory. His passion for both the people who dwell in every nation and also for the reclamation and transformation of the places in which they dwell will be unstoppable. The intensity of God's desire to dwell with us is contrasted with the intensity of His holiness, which requires distance from us until all things are restored and made new. The earth must be transformed into a resting place for the Lord that He might dwell here with His people forever (see Revelation 21:3).

The end of our story in this age of history is the glorious moment in which heaven comes down to the earth—the return of Jesus in blazing holiness and incomparable majesty.

It is critical to reassert that God's desire is not that any should perish but that all should repent and come to the knowledge of the truth, that all men might be saved from the judgment, shaking and the wrath to come (see 2 Peter 3:9). This is why Joel's prophecy makes it so clear that God's intention behind the outpouring of the Spirit on the saints and His worldwide distribution of extraordinary signs and wonders is not that people would be condemned, but that they would be saved to enjoy the glories of life within the family of God, under the dynamic rule of Christ the King.

Global Salvation for All Who Respond to the Lord

The goal of the global outpouring of glory is the salvation of every human being who sees and hears and believes: "And it shall come to pass that whoever calls on the name of the LORD shall be saved" (Joel 2:32a). All of the terrors and the signs in the heavens and on the earth will occur for one purpose: to provoke the human race to cry out to the Lord for their salvation. But will this phenomenal global outpouring result in a corresponding global response of repentance? Not according to Joel's prophecy. Joel tells us that a remnant will respond and be saved (see Joel 2:32b). What about the rest of humanity? How will they respond?

Because this storm of glory will prove to be greater than every revival in church history combined, we tend to romanticize both the scope and the cost. Again, we are talking about a revival similar to the First or Second Great Awakening, but far greater in intensity and global in scope. Because this revival is beyond our ability to imagine, we can trivialize the subject or dismiss it entirely. Or, in our romanticizing, we can view such a move of God's presence and power as a solution to our frustrations with the Church. Impatient with the delay, we forget that God is continually at work to prepare the way, and that He is intent on preparing His Church for His Day and the rage that He sees clearly in the human heart. He is not ignorant nor is He sentimental about the storm of revival on the horizon and what it means for His people.

Therefore, the best thing we can do is to encourage each other to be prepared and to set our hearts toward a deeper engagement with the leadership of the Lord. The Lord's leadership of our lives ensures that we can meet the challenges of this future intensity with sweet simplicity. Our small and simple yes of obedience to the Lord sets us on a very sure foundation in uncertain times. We can and must develop a culture of patience in waiting on the Lord and a persistence in engaging with Him as we grow in love and resolve, staying faithful in prayer over many decades.

The Nations Awakened and Provoked

Once we understand that it is hard to imagine a global revival and its impact on the nations (and the response of the peoples), it is helpful for us to learn the lessons of the past to understand our future. The book of Acts is the easiest way to begin to understand the prophecy of Joel and the dramatic events that are described in Joel 2 and many other passages. The book of Acts is a local, citywide preview of a global outpouring of the Spirit and the reaction of the nations to it. It also helps me to think of the book of Revelation—which intimidates many believers who struggle to read and understand it—as the "end-time book of Acts on a global scale."

However, it seems to me that Christians who utilize the book of Acts as a model for their ministry and the Spirit's activity un-intentionally emphasize only the positive elements of the book. They ignore the more intense elements of Luke's account. Yet I find the exact opposite to be true of the book of Revelation, where believers see John's encounter with Jesus about the future to be mostly negative or intense and cannot comprehend the beauty and victory within its pages. Therefore, we need both accounts as a template for our global future. We need to absorb and contextualize both the negative and intense elements of the storyline along with the very hopeful, very beautiful and victorious aspects of the future.

As we examined earlier in Acts 2:16–21, Peter made refer-ence to Joel 2:28–32 to explain the outpouring of the Holy

Spirit on the city of Jerusalem. Again, he was not saying about the Pentecost outpouring, "Joel's prophecy is now fulfilled and finished." He was helping the Jews of the city understand what was happening to them in light of that promise. In other words, Peter was saying, "This is the *beginning* of that," and what is yet to come in fullness according to the promise of Joel 2–3 was just then beginning to unfold. The kind of outpouring of the Spirit in glory and power that will happen across the whole earth was happening to a lesser (but very profound) degree on a citywide level in the second chapter of Acts.

How did Jerusalem respond? As Joel promised, the outpouring of the Holy Spirit, the activation and engagement of the people of God, and the power and glory of God on the Gospel led to thousands of salvations in Jerusalem (three thousand initially) with many being added daily to their numbers (see Acts 2:40–47). However, the glory and the power of God on the church also produced fear in everyone in the city and great rage and persecution from the city leadership (see Acts 5). Yet in the midst of the persecution there was grace for prayer, great boldness and deep unity.

As the storm of glory exploded in Jerusalem, Psalm 2 became a source of hope and comfort for the early Church (see Acts 4:25–26). The leaders of the early Church were not surprised by the response of Jerusalem's leadership to the power of the Holy Spirit. They understood that the pronouncement of the arrival of the true King of Israel, punctuated by both His resurrection and the outpouring of the Holy Spirit—would have the effect of enraging the leaders of the city and inciting them to persecute the Church. Therefore, they expected the backlash and the anger, and were prepared to endure the persecution with confidence and faith.

How do you understand and tell the story of the book of Acts? What is the nature and the impact of the Gospel you preach? Do you focus mostly on the power and positive dimensions, romanticizing the glory and ignoring or seeking to escape from the trouble? Or do you focus more on the negative dynamics, therefore shying away from the message and the power of God because of the mess that it makes?

Movements of the Holy Spirit

Another burning question: How can we be so bold and so confident as to expect that the kind of revival that Joel predicted is coming in our lifetime?

There is an unknown and profoundly sovereign dimension to revivals of any kind. No one can make God move or pour out His Spirit upon a region or a people. The sovereign nature of revival and the history of movements of the Holy Spirit can cause leaders and church attendees to have a laissez-faire attitude toward the subject. If revival is entirely in God's hands, why should we concern ourselves with such things? What relevance does this subject have for my everyday life if nobody knows whether or not this will be happening in the near, or even faraway, future?

Like the subject of the Second Coming, the subject of revival may be very important, but many of us fail to find it urgent enough to warrant much of our time and attention. Nevertheless, I believe that the pertinent questions are: When is this revival going to happen? Is it possible that this could impact our lives in our time?

To understand revival and the future outpouring of the Holy Spirit, it may be instructive to look back at the past few hundred years of our history.

In 1722, as the Enlightenment was beginning to come to full bloom in Europe, a wealthy young nobleman and landowner named Count Nikolaus Ludwig von Zinzendorf opened his estate to provide asylum and Christian community for religious minorities that had been oppressed by the Catholic Church. A handful of young Moravian Protestants found their way to his door, and together they founded a new settlement they named Herrnhut, which means, "Under the Lord's Protection" or "The Lord's Watch." It was on this land, after a significant outpouring of the Holy Spirit on August 13, 1727, that Zinzendorf and his Moravian community began to give themselves to a night-and-day prayer watch that would continue for a century. Zinzendorf longed for a passionate and pietistic "religion of the heart" that would warm the cold expression of rational religious thought that had overtaken the Reformation as a byproduct of Enlightenment philosophy. These Herrnhut prayer watches became the source of the spiritual power that lit fires of mission and revival from England and the colonies of America to the ends of the earth.

The earliest Protestant mission initiatives were born out of these prayer watches. Sixty years before the pioneering missionary to India William Carey, who was himself inspired by Moravian missionary zeal, seventy young Moravians from this community of six hundred answered the call to take the Gospel to the ends of the earth, famously declaring that their aim was that "the Lamb would receive the reward of His suffering." The flame of night-and-day prayer sparked the explosion of Protestant missions over the next three hundred years. This was one more dramatic illustration of the effectiveness of continual intercessory prayer. The spread of Christianity historically has been fueled by prayer, from the prolonged prayer in the Upper Room before Pentecost and onward over the millennia since then.

The Moravian prayer watches and their fruit in the lives of the missionaries that came out of them had a dramatic impact on John Wesley, founder of the Methodists in England, and also on the First Great Awakening, during which the fires of revival swept across the American colonies and Great Britain. For every revival or dramatic outpouring of the Holy Spirit's power that has had an impact on a region—I think of Cornwall, Wales, the Hebrides islands, Cane Ridge in Kentucky, Azusa Street in California and many more—there is an underlying story of prayer and intercession. To think that it all started with one small but persistent night-and-day prayer watch in Germany.

There is, then, throughout church history, a dynamic connection between prayer, missions and revival. However, such concerted prayer efforts are sporadic and rare. When they spring up among the people of God, nonstop prayer produces a profound yearning for God and a zeal for the lost—and a subsequent missionary outreach that is fueled by an outpouring of the Holy Spirit.

What is noteworthy about this pattern of divine activity is that Jesus spoke of night-and-day prayer, unprecedented missions and revival in Jerusalem as the global and ecclesial activities that would precede His return.[5] Jesus establishes the pattern in His teaching prior to the book of Acts, and then later church history illustrated this interrelationship between prayer, missions and the power of God. All of this serves as a preview of the conclusive expression of what the prophets and Jesus foretold—a final, global movement of prayer, worship and missions that will unleash the most widespread revival in all of recorded history, followed by the most important one of all: the Jerusalem revival that heralds the coming of the Messiah in the fullness of His glory to that city to rule.

This, then, is the great question that is set before this generation: Are we living in the generation of the Lord's return? We live in a day in which there are more expressions of night-and-day prayer than ever before. We have more prayer gatherings, prayer meetings, houses of prayer and other expressions of continual prayer than at any other point in church history. One leader privately confided to our team that, in his decades of tracking prayer in the Church, he had never seen more expressions of corporate prayer than he has over the past decade. According to his tracking, he estimated that there might be over 10,000 houses of prayer across the earth at this very moment. Mission leaders express the same enthusiasm over the current expressions of missionary work that are happening worldwide. There has never been a time quite like ours for evangelism and the spread of the Gospel.

This includes the work of the Gospel, prayer and missions within Israel and Jerusalem. Night-and-day prayer has resumed in Jerusalem for the first time since the era of King David. The great question of the imminence of the Lord's return is informed by the developments in these movements of prayer, in missions, and in Israel. Jesus Himself connected them to His return. It could be the case that such an unprecedented volume of prayer, outreach through missions, and gospel impact in Israel are signaling the long-awaited global revival. The Spirit invites us to take note and to begin to prepare our lives accordingly, for revival always follows prayer, and rage always follows revival.

If one night-and-day prayer meeting in Germany in the eighteenth century was the spark that ignited the flame of one of the most significant revivals and mission movements in history, what might God be preparing to do on the earth with perhaps 10,000 night-and-day prayer meetings? The fact that missionaries are reporting an unprecedented increase in salvations, signs and wonders across the earth and that continual prayer is going up (even in Jerusalem itself) forces us to face the personal implications. The Holy Spirit invites us to take note and to begin to prepare our lives accordingly. The storm of revival is on its way.

5

The Coming Storm of Rage

Why do the nations rage, and the people plot a vain thing? The kings of the earth set themselves, and the rulers take counsel together, against the LORD and against His Anointed, saying, "Let us break Their bonds in pieces and cast away Their cords from us."

Psalm 2:1–3

Scripture and redemptive history provide a clear picture of the great dilemma: The more God interacts in direct ways with the people of the earth, the more people resist, rebel and rage against Him. Our God is a God who loves people and longs to be with them in intimate, dynamic ways. Since the fall of man in the Garden of Eden, however, God's interactions with human beings have been greatly influenced by what Paul the apostle called "the mystery of iniquity" (2 Thessalonians 2:7 KJV). The great mystery that Paul is addressing in that verse is the mystery of fallen humanity's hidden rage against his Maker. It is neither logical nor rational that human beings should hate and reject a God who is as kind, merciful, loving, patient and beautiful as the God of the Bible. Yet for millennia people have carried in their hearts the seeds of deep contempt toward God's sovereignty, power and even His very existence. Since the Fall in the Garden of Eden, the nearer that God comes to the human race, the more angrily and intensely the human race pushes Him away.

This is less true of the transformed man or woman who, over time, becomes filled with the Word of God and the Spirit of God. Transformed men and women become ambassadors of the power and the righteous otherness of God in the midst of a fallen, broken and unrighteous world. This is one of the ways that the light of Jesus shines in the midst of the darkness of the world, the "true Light which gives light to every man" (John 1:9).

The problem lies in the fact that, although the light has come into the world, people love the darkness rather than the light because their deeds are evil (see John 3:19–20). That summarizes the roots of human rage and anger against God (and human self-justification). We justify our fears and biases. We find comfort and safety in our opinions and prejudices. We want the freedom to follow our hearts and become what we believe to be our true and authentic selves.

The person who has been transformed by God's love can then become an irritant for others because the light of God rubs against the love of darkness that men stubbornly cling to. This can lead to conflict, frustration and awkward or difficult social dynamics for the individual who has been changed by the power of God.

Yet we rarely see on an individual level the expression of rage that the Bible declares will be a part of the Christian experience.[1] How do the men and women that Jesus spoke of, the ones who love darkness and who therefore hate the light, become over time entire nations that rage against the living God, His Son and His Church? How is it possible that the nations of the earth could become unified in their anger against the God of Israel? Again, the issue is connected to power—who has it, how it is expressed and how that affects the way every man, woman and child on the earth lives their lives.

David and the Rage of the Nations

In his second psalm, King David gives us an astonishingly vivid picture of our future by describing a period of global collaboration against the God of Israel. This psalm is an ancient song about the nations' rage. It portrays a terrifying snapshot of the climactic moment in the millennia-long journey humankind has taken to deliberately walk far away from God. The great surprise that David unveils is something more than "mankind hates God" or "individuals rage against God within their souls." This is a song about the actions that the nations take together from a place of *unified* rage—calculated, coordinated rage that comes against God from everywhere on earth at one moment in history. This, then, is a very different scenario for the Church to wrestle with. How can it be? How can the nations become unified in their calculated rage against God? What does it mean for the Church?

David's song makes a bold declaration about the future, envisioning a moment in time in which the nations of the earth, unified in their seething rage against God, are about to erupt into a boiling storm. The specific reason and object of their anger is God's Anointed, or His chosen and appointed King.

The implication from the text is that this is a song about the coming of the Messiah of Israel, the promised son of David, who would rule over Israel with great power and authority, before whom the nations of the earth would bow down (see Isaiah 2:1–4). By divine decree, His rule extends beyond Israel to all the nations of the earth. The ancient Hebrews understood that their Messiah's dominion would be "from sea to sea" and that it would extend "to the ends of the earth" (Psalm 72:8). Within David's song of the nations' rage, it seems as if the kings of the nations around the world understand well the intentions of God and His chosen King.

David professed in his song that the coming of the Messiah was glorious news for the earth. In Psalm 72, David sang of the Messianic King's righteous and just rule, bringing justice to the poor and shattering the power of the oppressors of the earth. He will be the one to bring true peace to the earth by filling it with the glory of the God of Israel; all the people of the earth will be blessed by His leadership, and therefore bless His name (verses 17–18). Both prayer for Him and praises about Him will be lifted up repeatedly (verse 15) as He helps those who have no helper and serves the poor and oppressed worldwide. Therefore, as in Psalm 2, the appointment of the Messiah to his rightful rule is cause for rejoicing and celebration rather than scorn and war.

David contrasts the era of global peace and unity during which the poor have a compassionate advocate in the righteous King of Israel[2] (and during which all the peoples will pray for Him continually as He rules by the power and anointing of the Holy Spirit[3]) with the preceding era of false peace and safety,[4] which will have been a time of globally unified rage against God before the coming of His Messiah. During the time of unified rage, the kings will have oppressed the poor and the helpless[5] while seeking to accumulate more power to overthrow God's plans.

There is a coming day, according to David, when powerful and corrupt kings will set themselves against the Lord and His Anointed King. During that coming day, rulers will take counsel together to break God's restraints over their actions. What David writes about here is hard for us to imagine, because it describes a future in which there will be a coordinated, calculated rebellion across the earth against the God of Israel and His chosen King. For this to come to pass, a few other things would have to be true, such as the following:

- The kings and rulers of the nations of the earth would have to take seriously the existence, immanence and power of the God of Israel.
- These kings and rulers would be enraged because they believe that the God of Israel presents a clear and present threat to their established power and autonomy.
- The kings and rulers of the nations of the earth would have heard the news about the coming of Jesus to rule as the One chosen by God to be the rightful King of Israel.
- The kings and rulers of the earth would be enraged because they would believe that He represents a real threat to their autonomy, power and value systems.
- Raging and desiring to break free from the "chains" of the God of Israel and His chosen King, the kings and rulers of the earth would unite in a plot to overthrow the One who is coming to rule.

These statements represent astonishing developments! It is hard for us to imagine kings, rulers, governors and presidents agreeing on anything at all unless it conforms to their preestablished political ideologies and national interests. Yet David is telling us that a threat is coming to their power and authority that will transcend their political parties and ideologies, a common enemy that will unite them all in rage and rebellion.

Psalm 2 serves as a critical introduction to the drama of the coming of Jesus, because it provides a clear picture of events that precede His return. Lying beneath the narrative of this song is an implication that is stated more explicitly elsewhere, namely, "How will the kings and rulers *know*?"

How will they know about the God of Israel, His intentions and plans, His appointment of Jesus to the throne of Israel and the coming of Jesus to take the throne? What is the answer to the rhetorical question at the beginning of the psalm: "Why do the nations rage?" (Psalm 2:1). David has begun his song near the climax of the story, somewhere just before the moment when the God-man, Jesus of Nazareth, breaks through the sky in fire and vengeance.[6] He begins in the middle of the action, when kings are raging and rulers are making plans to overthrow God. David is not asking why to open up a mystery for the reader; he is asking, "Why would the nations engage in such a hopeless, laughable endeavor?"

This is why the rhetorical question is followed by the mocking laughter of God from the heavens—this uproar is the work of ants seeking to overthrow a mountain. The psalm is a call to kings and rulers worldwide to bow down and give their unreserved allegiance to the coming King of Israel, to cease their foolish raging against the inevitable moment when God will hand over their nations to Jesus when He returns, for they are rightfully His:

"I will declare the decree: The LORD has said to Me, 'You are My Son, today I have begotten You. Ask of Me, and I will give

You the nations for Your inheritance, and the ends of the earth
for Your possession. You shall break them with a rod of iron;
You shall dash them to pieces like a potter's vessel.'"

Psalm 2:7–9

By beginning in the middle, David thrusts the audience right
into the fire of the rage of nations against God and their rejection of His plans and desires. Yet for the modern reader, the
question remains, How did they know God's plans?

Jesus and the Persecution of the Church

Another aspect of the nations' rage is found in Matthew 24
where, as with David's psalm, Jesus gives us a picture of a future
in which all of the nations will be unified in their hatred—this
time their hatred of the Church.

> "Then they will deliver you up to tribulation and kill you, and
> you will be hated by all nations for My name's sake. And then
> many will be offended, will betray one another, and will hate
> one another. Then many false prophets will rise up and deceive
> many. And because lawlessness will abound, the love of many
> will grow cold. But he who endures to the end shall be saved.
> And this gospel of the kingdom will be preached in all the world
> as a witness to all the nations, and then the end will come."

Matthew 24:9–14

In Jesus' description of the future, the Church will be despised
across the globe because the name of Jesus will be so despised.
The association of Jesus with His Church will put Christians
at risk of tribulation or worse—being killed outright.

107

Without telling them how the storm will begin, Jesus warns His disciples of a future storm of anger and rage against Christians (verse 9). Storms of hatred and persecution have burst against the Church in the past and are happening around the world in various places today, but there has never been a time during which *all* nations have been unified in their animosity toward the Church.

Persecution is not our favorite subject to think, study or pray about. Especially in the Western world, we rarely preach or write about it because it does not seem to be an imminent threat to us. We may become disturbed when we hear about persecution happening elsewhere, but in general we feel safe from it. Therefore, we have learned to think of "tribulation" and "the hatred of the nations" in either a generically spiritualized sense ("People generally hate God and the Gospel") or dismissively ("This hatred is speaking of events in the first century, not the future").

Our failure to think about Matthew 24 in a straightforward manner is part of a pattern. We fail to apply other words from Jesus to ourselves, too. In His Sermon on the Mount, Jesus announced, "*Blessed* are those who are persecuted for righteousness' sake. . . . *Blessed* are you when they revile and persecute you, and say all kinds of evil against you falsely for My sake" (Matthew 5:10–11, emphasis added). In general, we prefer not to think about persecution, yet Jesus presents it in this passage as a great blessing to believers when it happens.

To begin to align our hearts with His, we must read the rest of the beatitudes from the Sermon on the Mount. These eight "blessed are" statements culminate with the one about being persecuted, almost as if being persecuted for righteousness' sake proves that one is living out the truth of the previous seven statements. In other words, it seems as if, in this progression, someone who embodies the beauty of Jesus so thoroughly will provoke a very negative reaction from those who do not. Your persecutors feel threatened by Jesus' life expressed through your life; they love the darkness rather than the light of the righteousness of Jesus and His ways.

On a global scale, the widespread antagonism toward the Church will be a sign, too. Something will have happened within the Church that threatens and challenges the authority of the nations, and the powers of the earth will want to put a stop to it. People and nations will not have hated the Church until they see the true status and dominant ascendency of the Church and are threatened by its message.

This, of course, is not the present state of affairs. We could label the current relationship between the nations of the earth and the worldwide Church as simply *indifferent*. As George Bernard Shaw (and later on, Elie Wiesel) famously observed, the opposite of love is not necessarily hatred, but rather indifference. At present, the world by and large neither believes the message of the Church nor feels pressed to accept Jesus as anything more than an enlightened teacher and wise sage. The earth continues to turn on its axis, and individuals carry on with their busy lives without giving a thought to the ideas and affairs of the Church around the world.

The prophetic Scriptures and the words of Jesus indicate a future in which something catalytic occurs to shift millions from indifference to hatred. Hatred is a form of passion that fuels action, often in reaction to perceived threats that evoke fear, pain or loss. The combined last-days hatred of the nations of the earth will be a powerful indicator that the Church has become a threat to the well-being of those whose power is defined in earthly terms. The Church will have arisen to do something powerful and significant in a unified way across the earth.

The global persecution and hatred of the Church will turn out to be some of the best news we could receive regarding the future of the Church. It will be a sign of great blessing on the Church and an indicator of great victory for the Gospel and the glory of God.

In the days to come, when the nations dramatically align themselves against the Church, they will have come to understand the Church to be a threat to their hard-won power and their influence over the people. What else could evoke such passionate rage? The Church will be a threat to them—and they will be *afraid* of the Church. Fear makes people fight.

As the nations see the results of the Gospel being preached to all the world, they will perceive the Church and our returning King as a true and legitimate threat to the established powers and rulers of the nations. This is an indication that the global impact of the message of the Kingdom of God will be greater in every way than any outreach the Church has known in the past. Jesus is telling us here about the glory and the power of His plan through the Church in the days to come: The message of the good news of the Kingdom of God is going to have global impact with a global witness of the coming King. Throughout the Word of God, we can see this promise of messengers filling the nations with the witness of the Gospel. The proclamation of Jesus in Matthew 24:14 is a promise of the greatest missions movement in the history of the Church before He returns.

There is the difference between the evangelistic Gospel that is being shared around the world today and the message that Jesus promised would fill the earth before His return: the Gospel of forgiveness and mercy from God related to our sins is a message preached to individuals; the "Gospel of the Kingdom" is a political message regarding the returning, rightful King of Israel and His intention to conquer and rule all of the nations of the earth. It is a message that encompasses nations, cultures, economies and every ethnic group and language group on earth. The breadth and scope of this message is unprecedented in the history of missions; the subsequent impact and resulting global persecution will be far beyond anything we have seen before in Church history. If Matthew 24:9–14 gives us a clear picture of the final missions movement of this age (and a message attached to that missions movement that is unlike any in power and scope that have come before), then Psalm 2 is the evidence of the impact of the message on the kings, rulers and people across the world.

The Valley of Decision: The Great Crisis for Every Nation

What David and Jesus foretold is brought to vivid life in the book of Revelation, specifically in chapters 17 and 18, which depict an end-of-the-age religious/economic entity known as the great harlot, or Babylon, riding on a scarlet beast with seven heads. She is shocking in her wickedness and power. We find her engaging in exactly what Jesus prophesied in Matthew 24. She will deliver the Church up to tribulation and kill the saints: "I saw the woman, drunk with the blood of the saints and with the blood of the martyrs of Jesus. And when I saw her, I marveled with great amazement" (Revelation 17:6).

The woman represents the collective group that Jesus spoke of, who would persecute the Church and kill the saints and martyrs: "Come, I will show you the judgment of the great harlot who sits on many waters, with whom the kings of the earth committed fornication, and the inhabitants of the earth were made drunk with the wine of her fornication" (Revelation 17:1–2). This entity who will rise up at the end of the age will

111

have become intimately acquainted with the kings of the earth *and* the inhabitants of the earth.

This imagery is almost beyond us in the 21st century. We may be Christians all our lives and never give much thought to these two chapters in John's Revelation. The entity in view there is the ancient city of Babylon reborn into a new and modern context, and an angel tells John that this entity will threaten the entire human race. Babylon is a central and important part of the redemptive story that God wants to tell because Babylon represents what lies at the heart of the human race, separated from God. What kind of world did humankind build after eating of the fruit of the Tree of the Knowledge of Good and Evil? A world without God, one characterized by the bitter fruit of human potential, and it is still growing to the height of its powers.

Babylon raises a painful question for us, the question of who and what we really are. This is not a question we enjoy being asked. What is the nature of humanity apart from God? Is humankind basically good, decent and noble? Or are we wicked, worthless, good for nothing except rage and spite and lust and greed? Apart from God, people answer that question by forming their own opinions of themselves, both high and low, fueled by pride, sentimentality and self-righteousness.

The new Babylon at the end of the age represents for us all a definitive answer from heaven. The great city is the eschatological personification of humanity, unchained and free to build and destroy. Babylon represents the ability of man to finally be his own god, with all of the wealth, religious permission, and potential to realize his every sinful ambition. The end of the book of Revelation shocks us in its graphic portrayal of a global capital of religion, finance and corruption. There will be no limit to its reach, and no end to its potential—which will have come at a staggering price, the blood of the saints.

The world powers, it seems, will have been more than willing to pay this price. They will have sacrificed the faithful and upright Bride of Christ without remorse in order to secure for themselves a future without God. Those of us who consider ourselves part of the Bride of Christ need to allow His light to reveal what we need to know in order to thrive and prosper in these days ahead.

There is another city, and it also represents an answer from heaven: the new Jerusalem. God will fill His holy city with the redeemed.[7] This glorious city is the eschatological statement of man's worth to God and the dignity and beauty of our destiny in Him. It is God's eternal home with His family, and the fulfillment of His burning desire to bring us all together again. In the new Jerusalem, the members of the human race will find out what they are made for, and they will enjoy full freedom to enjoy God according to His original design.

The book of Revelation puts the future on display: two cities, two peoples, two powerful ideas regarding what this world should be; each side possessing a strong sense of destiny, spirituality and morality. Between a great harvest of souls and a great falling away from the faith, we find a last great migration toward one of two places: the new Jerusalem above or the new Babylon below, the heavenly city to come or the doomed earthly city. These two cities and their populations will serve as a sort of final expression of the two trees of the garden: life with God and, in opposition, the knowledge of good and evil apart from God.

Everyone—*everyone*—on earth will have to make a difficult and final choice regarding which people they will identify with, which God (or god) they will serve and upon which truth they will ultimately stand.

The great crisis at the end of the age is like a fragile precipice upon which every person on earth will stand, overlooking the fateful "valley of decision." Each and every one must choose which God/god they will serve and which Kingdom/kingdom they want to be associated with. The prophet Joel wrote about this valley of decision:

> "Let the nations be wakened, and come up to the Valley of Jehoshaphat; for there I will sit to judge all the surrounding nations. Put in the sickle, for the harvest is ripe. Come, go down; for the winepress is full, the vats overflow—for their wickedness is great.
>
> "Multitudes, multitudes in the valley of decision! For the day of the LORD is near in the valley of decision. The sun and moon will grow dark, and the stars will diminish their brightness. The LORD also will roar from Zion, and utter His voice from Jerusalem; the heavens and earth will shake; but the LORD will be a shelter for His people, and the strength of the children of Israel."
>
> Joel 3:12–16

Revelation 17–18 gives us a mirror in which to view the truth about the human race apart from God—and motivation to avoid that outcome. Our fallen desires are opposed to His righteous desires for us. God wants to us to dwell with Him as part of His eternal family. But in our brokenness, we spurn Him, preferring to build a world without Him. We find ourselves in the middle of a cosmic, existential struggle to determine the fate of the human race and the kind of world we will possess and build. Is this world fundamentally ours to possess and to build in our own image? Or does it belong to the Lord, with the human race as His rightful possession and reflection of His image?

The final crisis at the end of the age—the storm of rage and rebellion against the Lord and against His Church—is the culmination of the collision of two colossal agendas. In the end, and eternally, only one can remain.

The rage of the nations against the saints represents the nations' rejection of God's agenda, which has been given voice through His Church. Psalm 2 and Matthew 24 give us a picture of a message filling the earth, one that the kings and peoples of the earth react to with fear, hatred and rage.

The progression is sobering: The message fills the earth by means of the proclamation of the Church, and this is followed by great hatred and rage from the nations of the earth as they react to that message—and to its enthusiastic reception by the multitudes. Important to note (and I will expand upon this later) is the fact that hatred and rage will by no means be the *only* reaction to the Gospel of the Kingdom proclaimed by the Church around the world.

A vast multitude of saints—many of them newly converted to the faith—will emerge victoriously from the time of "great tribulation," despite the hatred and rage of the nations at that time (see Revelation 7:9–17). Yes, great rage and hatred is coming—but it is coming because great glory and power is coming to the Church, resulting in the greatest harvest of souls into the Kingdom in all of history.

The Great Crisis Explodes: War against the Lamb

As the drama unfolds between the Church, the nations and Jesus Himself, something spurs an escalation in which the nations will be motivated to plan together and to act to thwart His agenda. Shockingly, Revelation 17 (as well as many other prophetic passages, such as Joel 3) portray the culmination of the nations' plotting and coordinated action, which shifts the action away from the persecution of the Church and toward the declaration of war against the Lamb of God Himself: "These will make war with the Lamb" (Revelation 17:14). Here is how Joel prophesied this terrible war of the nations against Jesus:

> Proclaim this among the nations: "Prepare for war! Wake up the mighty men, let all the men of war draw near, let them come up. Beat your plowshares into swords and your pruning hooks into spears; let the weak say, 'I am strong.'" Assemble and come, all you nations, and gather together all around. Cause Your mighty ones to go down there, O LORD.
>
> Joel 3:9–11

Two counter-narratives run parallel to one another throughout the book of Revelation. The first involves the activities of a mysterious and powerful figure whose wicked plans and schemes throw the nations into chaos and lawlessness as he rises to even greater power. In Revelation 13, he is revealed as the Beast (a wicked political and military leader). He joins with a second beast (a wicked spiritual leader) to establish a massive empire based in the Middle East. In this same chapter, we see the beast and his empire come to the fullness of his power over the nations. The end-time judgments of God that John witnessed and wrote about are primarily against this man, his empire and all who align themselves with him worldwide.

The second (but primary) narrative of the book of Revelation involves the activities of Jesus (the Lamb of God) as He brings history to His desired conclusion. As the Beast leads his empire, the Lamb leads His Church to stand against injustice and unrighteousness, to contend for the breakthrough of the Holy Spirit in power, and to engage in the greatest harvest of souls in human history. Revelation 17–19:10 are critically important passages, within the book of Revelation itself as well as throughout all of the prophetic Scriptures.

All of the great themes of Scripture and of the book of Revelation come together: the Lamb of God, who represents the pinnacle of all that men can be in Christ by the grace of God, and the Beast, who represents the pinnacle of all that men can be in rebellion and wickedness. It is the God-man against the Antichrist, the Bride of Christ against the harlot of Babylon, the new Jerusalem against the new Babylon; John's vision depicts the final stages of the plan of God and His story of man's redemption.

In chapters 1–3 of Revelation, the Father fully unveils Jesus to all believers and to all nations. He will return to the earth, and He will be seen by His own as the Son of man, the Bridegroom, the Lion of the tribe of Judah and the Root of David. To the nations, He will come as the Lamb of God, which speaks of something more than the atonement—the Lamb displays the magnificence of Jesus standing in the midst of the throne, in the midst of all the angels, and in the midst of all the peoples of the earth. He will be seen as "the brightness of [God's] glory and the express image of His person" (Hebrews 1:3) and the "image of the invisible God" (Colossians 1:15). The manner in which He will be revealed in the center of the throne—the center of the universe—declares in a powerful way how He sees Himself and How He wants to be known.

Jesus as the Lamb of God is the core message the Father wants to declare to the nations prior to His return. He wants the primary revelation of His Son to the lost to be the expression of sacrifice, mercy and tenderness in dealing with any who would turn and repent of their sin. This revelation of the core reality of who Jesus is will be a great comfort and anchor to the Church in the coming storms, as well as a great invitation and witness to the nations of the earth before Jesus returns. The Body of Christ will express the Lamb-like humility and tenderness of Jesus as a powerful witness to the true heart of Jesus before He returns.

The revelation of Jesus, the Lamb of God, makes the most complete statement in the Bible about the worth of Christ. By showing us Jesus as a Lamb, the Father tells us *how* Jesus is worthy (the slain Lamb is trustworthy), *why* Jesus is worthy (the meek and lowly Lamb is humble), and *what* it looks like for Jesus to walk out Lamb-like leadership in His desire to serve the nations. Jesus is worthy because of who He is; only He has the capacity to rule the world. Jesus is the safest, most trustworthy and most able leader. His right to govern the nations of the earth does not come from His role as Creator but rather from His role as the incomparably humble Servant of all.

The scandal of the book of Revelation is not that the Lamb is enraged, but that the nations are exposed in their wickedness by becoming enraged at a Lamb so lovely and lowly.

Summary: The True Nature of Man Unveiled

From the psalms of David, through the prophets, the gospels and the book of Revelation, we can view a picture of the nations' rage in the face of their great crisis. The rage of men against God has been simmering and seething under the surface for many millennia, but at some point in the future it is going to boil over in full view of all the peoples on the earth. Something powerful and catalytic will push the nations from their hidden, individual anger and hatred into a collective, calculated, unified rage that results in open war against God, His Son and His Church. What will be coming from heaven—which we examined in the previous chapter—will be coming by God's initiative and in His timing in order to provoke and expose the nations in their hidden rage and rejection of His agenda.

The prophet Jeremiah declared,

"Therefore prophesy against them all these words, and say to them: 'The Lord will roar from on high, and utter His voice from His holy habitation; He will roar mightily against His fold. He will give a shout, as those who tread the grapes, against all the inhabitants of the earth. A noise will come to the ends of the earth—for the Lord has a controversy with the nations; He will plead His case with all flesh. He will give those who are wicked to the sword,' says the Lord.

Thus says the Lord of hosts: 'Behold, disaster shall go forth from nation to nation, and a great whirlwind shall be raised up from the farthest parts of the earth.'"

Jeremiah 25:30–32

At the heart of the coming crisis, we will find that it is not the people's rage against God that is the driving force of the escalating drama, but God Himself, who has a "controversy with the nations" and will therefore "plead His case with all flesh." How merciful and compassionate is the God of Israel, how slow to anger, rich in love and kindness toward the stubborn, the lost and the rebellious. He will present every person on earth with an underserved choice, and time to make that choice. God will put His beauty, the righteousness of His Kingdom, and the hearts of His people, the Church, on full display.

The valley of decision will include powerful, wicked, oppressive kings and rulers, world powers who despise the God of Israel, His Son and His ways. God will have allowed these powerful kings and rulers to grow in power, while also displaying His own power and love for all the nations to see. He will send His Son as a Lamb, filled with kindness and mercy, desiring that all men would repent from their rebellion, be saved by His grace and come to know Him fully (see 1 Timothy 2:4).

119

We can better understand why things will happen the way that Scripture describes when we see clearly the sober picture of what the human race is really like apart from God. The plea that King David makes in Psalm 2:10 to the kings and rulers of the earth is "be wise." The persistent human problem is that, in every era of history, some are wise, some are foolish and some are wicked. The wise fear the Lord and obey His commands, the foolish are a mixture—sincerely intending to do well but not making good decisions—and the wicked are fixed on their own agendas, to the exclusion of the righteous agenda of the Lord. The coming, God-ordained crisis is meant to vindicate the wise, to allow the foolish time to repent and receive instruction, and to remove altogether the wicked who refuse to repent. The God of Israel desires to fill the earth with the wise, in order to plead with the foolish and expose the wicked.

In the scriptural passages explored in this chapter, we saw how the kings and rulers of the nations will rage at God with fear and hatred in the days to come. But what will shift them from indifference and scorn to rage and fear? What will cause them to take the Church so seriously in the coming days that they will begin to unite in a plot to persecute the saints and overthrow the Lamb? How is it possible that these incredibly wealthy and powerful leaders will be listening to the Church and preparing to confront Jesus?

The answer is found in the thing that all men covet—and go to war to obtain. That thing is *power*, and whether it is attained by means of wealth, influence, governmental authority or any other way, God is going to expose the powerlessness of the nations. The coming storm of rage will ensue when He shows them His superior power to execute His will. He will do so through the most breathtaking method possible: revival.

120

6

The Coming Storm of Political and Economic Disruption

We have a hard time grasping descriptions of the future that are global in scope and impact. The book of Acts can help us. It can serve as a template to help us understand the relationship between the divine activity that accompanies the outpouring of the Holy Spirit and the human response of rage and violent opposition. As I noted earlier, the book of Acts is like a localized version of the book of Revelation, and the book of Revelation is a global expression of much of what happens in the book of Acts.

Throughout the book of Acts, we see the progression: As the impact of the message and the power of God increases, it is followed by a corresponding increase of the intensity of persecution. We are not used to seeing this in our personal experience. We are accustomed to preaching a Gospel of individual salvation to our neighbors, and we expect those who hear it to respond either by believing it or dismissing it. We do not expect a rage-filled, violent response, at least in the Western world.

Yet as we have examined earlier, trouble begins when God adds powerful actions to the message, making it increasingly difficult for people to dismiss or ignore it. This is part of His agenda; He wants to confront the people of the earth, forcing them to grapple with Him and His Kingdom without violating their free will. In His great mercy, He breaks into human lives through His anointed, prophetic Church. He wants to display His transcendent love through a people who have been joined with His Spirit and who have been transformed into His likeness. Fundamentally, He greatly delights in showing the world His glorious Son through His imprint on the life of His transformed Bride.

Again, historically, the greater the degree of His self-revelation to the people of the earth in glory and power, the greater degree of their rage, resistance and rebellion toward Him. In His sovereignty, He always interacts with the human race in measured ways according to His meekness and tenderness (in many cases through the Church). Many people have wondered why God chooses to work through His Church rather than simply appearing in the sky in glory or speaking audibly to the masses. This question is asked in sincerity but with real naïveté regarding human nature: Underneath the surface within every fallen man who is separated from God lies a storm of rage.

In the book of Acts, we can trace the progression of the gospel message and the revival it engenders. Revival began in Jerusalem, and then, over the next few decades, progressed powerfully across the Roman Empire. At first, the gospel message touched individual lives, and soon its influence began to be felt in larger masses of individuals. When it began to make an impact on entire cities, local governments took note, because their power and influence was being threatened. This is when the reaction shifted from passive dismissal to active anger and violent rage. It is one thing to have handfuls of citizens following a religious message, but when the influence of that message threatens the power base of powerful governmental leaders, they react with alarm.

When the Gospel Impacts Politics and Government

From the beginning, the Gospel was a profoundly political proclamation. The apostles were not primarily proclaiming the good news of the forgiveness of sins and the message of individualistic salvation. They were proclaiming the coming of the Messiah and the implications of His coming. For the early Church, the Good News was the fulfillment of the most significant promise of the Scriptures, namely the resurrection and arrival of the appointed Messiah, the rightful King of Israel and therefore the King of all the nations of the earth. The fact that He had been raised from the dead made His true identity and appointed role inarguably glorious news for the early Church in Jerusalem, Judea and Samaria.

The Jerusalem council and the subsequent ministry of the apostle Paul opened the door fully for the early Church to take this politically charged good news to the pagans of the Roman Empire. They did not take a merely individualistic message of love and forgiveness. At the Jerusalem council, the apostle James quoted from the prophet Amos to convince the assembly of Jewish faithful that the turning of the Gentiles to the God of Israel had always been central to the Davidic promises (see Amos 9:11–12; Acts 15:16–18). Centuries earlier, the prophet

Amos had urged Israel not to cast aside the Davidic covenant because of the weakened condition of King David's line at that time. Amos proclaimed that the ruins of the government of David, which had fallen in Amos's day, would be fully rebuilt and restored, and that the pagan nations would make up a dynamic part of that government under the rightful King appointed by the God of Israel.

This is why James and the other apostles and elders decreed at the Jerusalem council that it should be easy for non-Jews to turn to God. They understood that the Gentiles who turned to the God of Israel and received the Holy Spirit did not need also to follow Jewish rituals and be circumcised. Religiously, culturally and politically, their conversion meant something more than becoming Jewish. Their conversion meant that they, even non-Jewish citizens of the Roman Empire, were submitting their lives to Jesus, the Jewish Messiah, and calling Him their true King. This was a threat to both the Roman rulers and the Jewish religious leaders. Thus, the first thing that the Jewish power base in Thessalonica shouted to the secular rulers of that city was this: "These who have turned the world upside down have come here too. Jason has harbored them, and these are all acting contrary to the decrees of Caesar, saying there is another king—Jesus" (Acts 17:6–7).

As explored in the previous chapter, Jesus Himself indicated that the nations of the earth would be filled with the message of the Gospel of the Kingdom before the end would come. He said that the proclamation of the Good News in the days to come will also result in more than individual salvations and the forgiveness of sins. He announced that the good news for the people of the earth in the coming days would include the full removal of injustice and oppression at the hands of unworthy kings and rulers of the earth. To cap it off, the ultimate unjust oppressor, the Antichrist, who will be the most powerful and wicked man in all of history, will be removed, and the true and rightful King will be enthroned. This King, appointed by the God of Israel, will reign on the earth from Jerusalem, and He will set society in order according to the truth.

We read the accounts in the book of Acts that Jesus' resurrection from the dead helped to serve notice to the powers of Rome that there was a greater power behind the Son of David, the rightful Jewish King. The miracles, signs and wonders served the same purpose; they proved that Jesus is the true King. Not to have had any displays of power would have left the message barren and empty. The Roman audience knew that Caesar had the most powerful and well-organized armies in the world at his command. To declare to them that a Jewish king had arrived and that he was the true King of all the nations—including Rome itself—was seditious. Yet large numbers of Gentiles began to give their allegiance to the rightful King of Israel, turning "the world upside down."

This is the other aspect of the Gospel and politics that we must consider: the unavoidable ramifications for governments when dynamic revival moves powerfully through a city or a region. The fact of this can be appreciated by simply looking at a hypothetical number of converts. In a democratic context, all it would take for a revival to overturn a government would be for the number of converts to grow to be more than 50 or 60 percent. Even in more oppressive contexts, rulers must acquiesce to some degree to the massive pressure that a large group of fervent Christians operating in unity can put on a wicked government.

For a moment, imagine your own city. If three hundred thousand people in your locality were suddenly converted powerfully with deep conviction and repentance, what could be the impact on how they would vote? Mass numbers of people can apply real pressure to the people in power. In the aftermath of the French Revolution, European powers lived in real fear of the possibility that the masses within their own nations would rise up to overthrow them violently. In reaction, these monarchies went to war against France to underscore their dominion and to send a message to their own people.

As a U.S. citizen, I have observed that there are few things that make people more nervous or upset than when they discover the deeply held religious beliefs or Christian associations of a possible candidate for president. People express themselves through media hit pieces and social media. They are "shocked" and "surprised" to discover that a candidate has a "hateful" or "oppressive" view of marriage, sexuality or other topics that are currently in the news.

They would be content for Christians in America to keep their faith private. ("That's nice for you, but leave me out of it.") But when the Gospel has corporate impact, suddenly the stakes change dramatically. I have observed that when Christianity has a potential influence on government at all, even minus the miraculous power of the Holy Spirit or widespread salvations, hidden rage rises up within the hearts of godless men and women. Suddenly, the gospel message and the morality of the Bible have the possibility of influencing public policy or shaping civil law.

Of course this dynamic becomes greatly amplified when an outpouring of the Holy Spirit accompanies the preaching of the Gospel, followed by signs, wonders and mass salvations of the lost. When wicked men with great power and influence are suddenly confronted with the loss of their control as a result of a power shift due to the move of the Holy Spirit in a region, they will react in much the same way as they did in the early chapters of the book of Acts. The Gospel would be preached with power, and a city would be shaken as suddenly many would come into the Kingdom. The political and spiritual leaders would ruthlessly act in response. Christians would be imprisoned, beaten and expelled from the city.

This brings me back to looking ahead. When we understand the pattern of the book of Acts—gospel preaching plus the power of the Holy Spirit unleashes a firestorm—suddenly David's psalm and Jesus' words make more sense to us. Yes, the Gospel of forgiveness of sins and the free gift of righteousness is beautiful, powerful and dear to our hearts. However, when the Gospel of the Kingdom is preached—the proclamation of the coming of the true King and the deliverance of an oppressed earth into His powerfully loving hands by the power of the Holy Spirit—and this is preached in the context of worldwide revival and a great harvest, the entrenched political powers will be enraged. The Church can expect much trouble and many trials.

This will bring real consequences for the people of God. That is why we must prepare our hearts and orient our lives so that we can endure with joy and perseverance in the days to come.

When the Gospel Shakes the Economy

Luke, the author of Acts, also shows us the impact of the Gospel and the power of the Holy Spirit on economics, finance and commerce, which can be far more violent than the reaction of governmental administrations.

By the time we come to Acts 19 and the revival of Ephesus, the upheaval caused by the gospel message has escalated to a new level. For the first time, the Gospel revival has become so disruptive that the very economy of Ephesus was turned upside down. The unusual signs and wonders, the number of salvations, and the depth of transformation were stirring the city up greatly. Yet when the Gospel touched *money*, something dramatic happened for the first time: Instead of opposing the gospel message by changing laws and removing the messengers, this city rioted and attempted to kill the messengers.

The economy of Ephesus at that time was built in part on the robust commerce that was connected with the temple of the goddess Artemis, or Diana, where temple prostitution, silver idols, sorcery and witchcraft prevailed. The economy, in other words, was built on idolatry, immorality and sorcery. When revival and the outpouring of the Holy Spirit crashed upon the city—this revival may have been the most potent and powerful move of the Spirit in church history—it overwhelmed the governmental and religious leaders, both Jews and Greeks, and it shook the economic base of the city itself. So many practitioners of magic came to believe in Jesus that they collectively burned over 5.5 million dollars' worth of books associated with their practice.[1] This gives us a powerful picture of the sheer number of people soundly converted by the power of the Gospel and the outpouring of the Holy Spirit upon Ephesus. This also gives us a picture of the depth of their conversions according to the power of the Holy Spirit. The fervency and sincerity of the new converts speaks of a significant release of power from the Spirit to bring deep, sudden change at the heart level.

The ramifications of this economic shaking were significant. The economic leaders of the city suffered the abrupt loss of a large number of former customers, who had now radically transferred their allegiance. Their change in personal values means that their economic decisions changed to reflect their new values.[2] This revival represented such a catastrophic loss of

business for the merchants of Ephesus that they quickly sum-
moned those who were dependent upon them for their liveli-
hoods, rallying them to rush to the city amphitheater to riot and
rage against the ministry of Paul. This open-air amphitheater
could hold up to 24,000 spectators. "Full of wrath," they cried
out in anger for two hours, "Great is Diana of the Ephesians!"
(Acts 19:28). Only by the intervention of the city clerk did Paul
and his coworkers narrowly avoid injury and death at the hands
of the crowd.

Why does this story matter to us? It is important because
in the days ahead, we need to wrestle with the cost of genuine
biblical revival. The cost may be high, but the reward is great.
As difficult as it is for us to imagine so many people responding
to the Gospel in such a short period of time that it disrupts the
commerce of a city, this kind of move of the Spirit lies ahead
for the Body of Christ across the world. So many lost souls will
repent and be saved that it will break economic systems that
have been built on darkness and sin. Along with the celebration of new life comes the sobering backlash from wicked and
powerful men with much to lose when their former customer
base leaves to follow Jesus. How will they provide for their families and employees without the revenue generated by wicked
means? This development would not be welcome to those who
experience such sudden, dramatic financial hardship, and they
would likely react quickly (with rage) to restore their economic
fortunes. How far will powerful and wealthy men go to maintain or restore their wealth and security?

In our modern world, governments and politicians possess significant power, but business corporations now possess far more
economic influence than some of the most powerful empires in
all of history. Therefore, it is not surprising to read in the book of
Revelation about the raging of economic powers after the mighty

move of the Spirit. There we see the scope of the Joel 2 revival: 21 judgments of God poured out upon the nations of the earth to bring men into deep repentance and heart transformation. These 21 judgments will be released over a very brief span of time at the end of the age—42 months, or 3½ years. Fourteen of these judgments *directly concern* money, economics and resources. God intends to get the attention of the nations to call them to repentance, and He is going to do it in the most dramatic way possible: He is going to shake the economics of the entire planet.

As often as we hear faith messages advertising the revival power of the Holy Spirit described in the first part of Acts 19, we rarely hear a call to prepare for the reaction of wicked men to it (again, according to what Luke described in the second part of Acts 19—the riot in Ephesus). We must reread Joel 2:28–31 and look toward our future with sober-minded boldness, leaving behind all romanticized sentimentality regarding the power of God.

When the Gospel touches institutions of political or economic power, men will react with fury. When the Gospel interferes with their moneymaking, powerful, wicked men will kill to preserve what they have acquired. The apostle James stated this clearly:

> Where do wars and fights come from among you? Do they not come from your desires for pleasure that war in your members? You lust and do not have. You murder and covet and cannot obtain. You fight and war. . . . Do you not know that friendship with the world is enmity with God? Whoever therefore wants to be a friend of the world makes himself an enemy of God.
>
> James 4:1–2, 4

The core issue of this war is our lust, or our agenda—our desire for the world to be as we want or need it to be. Apart from God, the pleasures of the human heart are comfort, safety, security and a covetous longing for more resources to secure those things in a manner we can control.

The three central statements about money and the human heart in the New Testament are these:

> Where your treasure is, there your heart will be also.
>
> Matthew 6:21

> "No one can serve two masters. Either you will hate the one and love the other, or you will be devoted to the one and despise the other. You cannot serve both God and money."
>
> Matthew 6:24 NIV

> The love of money is the root of all evil.
>
> 1 Timothy 6:10 KJV

The love of money—and the corresponding fear of lack—are powerful root causes of conflict on various levels. But Christians can have free hearts regarding money and resources because we know that our heavenly Father provides for us. We are able to serve Him using money as a tool to do so, rather than allowing money to be our master.

The world apart from God, however, does not have this freedom from economic fears and the lust for more money. Thus, in the world around us, we see growing fear and anger. In the context of such widespread anxiety, the Lord is about to shake the nations with a dramatic introduction of Holy Spirit power that will massively disrupt economies. We need to be prepared for such a time, because when the Gospel shakes the economy, it will affect us, too. Where will our hearts be?

131

The New Testament is uncompromisingly clear about our need to prepare for the days to come by getting free of all covetousness and fearful self-preservation. Jesus is going to shake the wealth of the earth to bring the nations into repentance, but His doing so will spark unprecedented rage and a spirit of murder. The greatest days of the Church are yet ahead, but so are some of the most troubling days for the Church.

How Then Shall We Live?

Our lives are not our own. The Holy Spirit is stirring His Church now, well in advance of the coming storm, to give us time to align ourselves with Jesus and His plan. What will you do? Will you contend for revival, regardless of the personal cost of doing so? Will you surrender yourself in the days to come, embracing everything as it is described in the Bible—accepting the glorious and difficult dynamics that come on the heels of revival?

Christians know that Jesus is committed to us; we are His Bride. He gives His life so that we can express what we were made for. Yet we are so weak. While I truly believe the things that I am writing about and want to give myself to the Word and to prayer so that I can engage with what the Spirit is doing today, I am all too aware of my humanity. I am inconsistent with spiritual disciplines. If my readiness for the future should depend solely on my ability and effort and dedication, then I will never be able to step into what the Lord is doing and will do.

However, if my hope is connected securely to the truth of Jesus' leadership and help, I will be able to follow Him straight into troubles and trials. This is what sets Christianity apart from every other religion on the planet—we have a God who fights for us. I have not been left to myself. I do not need to reach religious perfection, dutifully hoping to make Him happy. I have been saved by a God who is filled with joy as He sets Himself to the task of transforming me—a selfish, self-centered, impatient, prideful, distracted and often dull follower—into His likeness day-by-day. This is the biblical truth, and it is exhilarating to think about.

Moreover, He desires to take those of us whom He has made beautiful and put us on display out of mercy for the nations, so that they, seeing His handiwork, would repent and be saved. He is committed to the fulfillment of His plan, and His plan includes you and me. He loves us. He does not expect us to come to Him as already transformed, super Christians who are spiritual powerhouses. We can trust in His outrageous faithfulness, and He will make sure that we have what we need in the troubled days ahead.

You and I have a great future ahead of us. For our part, we must hold fast, wait on Him and not quit along the way. As we keep saying yes to Him, He responds to our sincere faith with so much more grace than we ever could have imagined, and in that grace, we will be able to do things that are far beyond what we ever could deserve.

PART TWO

THE CHURCH IN AN
ANTI-CHRISTIAN AGE

7

The Birth of the
Cultural Narrative

One of the contributing factors to our natural sluggishness in the face of the coming crisis is that we tend to be creatures of the moment. We deal mostly with what happens to be right in front of us; we are perpetually given to the "tyranny of the urgent." It is hard to prioritize a to-do list around prayer and intimacy with Jesus when there are real, seemingly more urgent demands on our lives.

Giving all of our attention to the many demands of our daily lives, we lose our focus on the larger storyline and our purpose in it. We close ourselves in. We even forget to use the quiet spaces in our lives to reconnect with the bigger picture, and we do not pay attention to the biblical and historical precedents that could inform our preparations for the future.

I find that many people live with a nagging unrest on the inside, an abiding sense that things are not right, but they are uncertain about what is wrong. Disconnected from the rock of the Word of God, they simply grumble and complain and process theories with friends, but they rarely gain insight enough to even think about the difficult days that lie ahead, possibly in the not-so-distant future. Certainly they do not grow in love and devotion for Jesus.

We live in a culture of words without depth or wisdom, and the unrest and uncertainty in our souls is, in large part, connected to the current cultural narrative. This narrative is driven by the arguments of self-righteous social justice crusaders who seek to suppress competing ideas—particularly Christian ones—through collective pressure that is designed to impute guilt and shame.

This cultural narrative is the current expression of the nations' rage against the Church. Loud voices seek to silence biblical concepts in favor of alternative ideas. Societal change is the goal, and revolt against traditional values is held up as a model for behavior. This cultural narrative feels new, but it has been growing for centuries.

The Christian World View and Humanistic Rage

Those with a Christian world view understand that the hand of a sovereign God shapes the course of history and that the Creator, the Maker of heaven and earth, has intentions, designs and plans for all that He has made. The intentions, designs and plans of God are inherently right, as Paul tells us, because the Potter has the right to use the clay for whatever purpose He wants (see Romans 9:14–29). In Romans 9, Paul makes a detailed case for the righteousness of God (in this case, meaning the "rightness" of God or the "right" ways and perfect leadership of God) as the Creator. Because He created and formed everything, His intentions must prevail. Creations must be subject to the One who created them.

When we live and think in ways that violate the divine design, we are rebelling against our Maker. This is unrighteous and destructive. By violating our divine design, we defile ourselves in sin, and we slowly destroy ourselves. By imposing our will in a way that harms the earth, we contribute to the destruction of another part of God's creation. By acting in a way that harms other people, we transgress the will of the God who created them. God holds His creation accountable for all of these areas related to His will.

Sinful human beings are troubled in particular by these two ideas in the Bible: man is subject to God (God is King), and man is answerable to Him (God is Judge). This is why so many people seek to make Jesus out to be only a teacher or a wise man. A person can respect and appreciate a wise man without giving his or her life to him. While praising the good teacher, the people can answer to something else (even themselves). If Jesus was only a man and a teacher, then people feel they can still live as they please. But calling Jesus King and Judge means they have to reckon with Him. We have to live as *He* desires and be held accountable to Him if we do not.

Humankind rages against this idea. The rebellion of the Fall caused a massive and tragic divorce from God, and from that time forward people have been going their own way and building up their own knowledge and power. Some of them tried to make things easier by deciding that God is not real, but once God has been removed from the picture, people must rely on their own souls. Then because it is difficult to rebel against one's very design—and against the soul's innate desire to know God—those who reject God eventually gather together. The old saying "misery loves company" typifies the pattern of history as sinful people join together to help one another resist God and contend with their consciences.

Two of the most important questions of human existence are "How do I know that God exists, and why should I be subject to Him?" In His great kindness, He looks to answer those questions through the prism of His love and mercy toward us. Because He loves us and pursues us and fights for us even when we are weak, immature and rebellious, we can receive power and help from Him to live our lives the way they were meant to be lived—connected to the knowledge of God, in deep agreement with Him and with what He wants.

We find, as we come to know Him, that He is not only a King to whom we are subject and a Judge to whom we are accountable, but also a Bridegroom. He *is* love, perfectly personifying and expressing love as He reveals Himself to us. This truth is the most exciting, liberating and joyful news we can receive about God. By identifying Himself as a Bridegroom, Jesus communicates to us that He is, as King David testifies, the One who has "the oil of gladness more than [His] companions" (Psalm 45:7). He is a joyful God who delights in His people. Knowing this changes our emotions toward Him as King and Judge.

When one does not know an earthly king or a judge, irrational fears, nervousness and defensiveness can arise in our hearts. I have been at traffic court and watched irrational anger erupt out of people around me. People hate being held accountable for breaking the law. This makes them want to blame the person with the black robe seated on the bench—who is just trying to do the job well and help enforce the law. That irrational anger toward decent people cannot compare to the irrational anger someone can feel toward God, who is far more powerful than any earthly judge.

Yet God looks to introduce Himself to rebellious people in mercy, compassion and kindness. Paul prayed that people's hearts would be directed toward the "love of God and the patience of Christ" (2 Thessalonians 3:5), and he affirmed that the "kindness of God leads you to repentance" (Romans 2:4 NASB). None of us deserves this kindness, but then God is not relating to us on the basis of what we deserve. He is relating to us on the basis of who *He* is. Jesus suffered and died even for those who never personally welcome His love and kindness, and He wants to know and enjoy that person forever.

Encountering Jesus the Bridegroom transforms how we feel and relate to Jesus the King and Judge. We move from fear and anger to confidence and tenderness. We shift from feeling compelled to do His will to *wanting* to do His will. As we grow more mature in love for Him, we grow increasingly confident about standing before Him one day. We discover that He wants to help us do well on the day of our judgment—and it fills our hearts with gratitude and appreciation. His generosity and kindness toward us are overwhelming.

This is the revelation of Jesus that will fill the earth at the end of this age. In the beginning, God revealed certain things about Himself. The end of the age closes with a different face of God, seen through His Son, Jesus. This serves to bring together everything we know about God so that we can stand with Him in confidence as He shakes the nations to bring them into the age to come, the age in which the Bridegroom, King and Judge will rule on the earth in view of all the peoples.

This is the story that God the Father is writing onto the hearts of every person in the human race. We broke away from the Father, the one who made us and who made the world so that He could live with us forever, but His response was not to retaliate or abandon us to our rebellion. Instead, He fought for us to be reconciled with Him, and He fought for the world to be cleansed and transformed. He did not want to allow our race to be destroyed and our world defiled. The story of man's redemption and the world's restoration is and will be the most glorious and beautiful story ever to unfold. We will enjoy God and enjoy one another as we retell His story for all eternity.

Raging against God to Redefine Human Freedom

From the Garden and the fall of man, the human race in rebellion has been seeking to write its own story. The human heart has fallen for the satanic deception that the story is about us, which is why the story of the human race as it has been told over the centuries has featured man as the hero. This old story has informed the current cultural narrative, which reflects what Western society wants to look like, what human morals should be, what justice and fairness should consist of, and what ideal freedom should be for people.

These are our cultural rules and norms that shape and define what we care about and how we should care about it. It would have worked out better if both the written laws and the unwritten social norms had flowed from a biblical ethic. God's righteous ways work best for our individual and our collective well-being. However, we find ourselves in an era of growing rage toward biblical morality and any form of external governance that is shaped by a Christian ethic. The way people think has shifted dramatically over the centuries, from a Catholic world view to a post-Christian one and then, in our era, an anti-Christian viewpoint. How did we get here?

As people began to organize themselves and gather into fortified cities and establish ancient societies and nations, they also began to seek to understand themselves and the world in which they lived. The root systems of society are always formed by human answers to questions about the nature of our existence and our relationship to our God and Maker. These answers in turn provided the framework for building governments and wielding power. They influenced decisions about sharing power cooperatively or seizing it in wars. It goes without saying that if a divine being has power over our lives and we are subject to His power, we will operate with different societal restraints than if we are the ones in power, essentially subject to ourselves.

At the heart of the Christian faith is the belief that there is a divine Author writing a glorious story about man's restoration and redemption. In the beginning, the story of humanity revolved around our Creator within the confines of the paradise He had established so that He could live with and enjoy His people in beautiful fellowship. Now the great promise set before all of the human race is the hope of our return to that setting, to dwell on a planet unencumbered by the chains of sin, rebellion and corruption. However, a counter-narrative has impeded the fulfillment of this promise.

Within the beating hearts of sinful people stirs the dream of a world without God, one in which humankind can be free to move into its "rightful" role of mastery over the world without interference from or subservience to any divine being. People want to achieve freedom not only from God's presence but also from His morality and laws. Our sinful human hearts cling to the hope that, freed from God's limitations, we might be able to enjoy the world more completely, and rule it. We object to God's right to rule, and we reject the authority of His Scriptures. Apart from God, each of us longs to write his or her own story.

Only if we understand the origins of today's cultural narrative can we navigate the social undercurrents that swirl around us. It is helpful for us to recognize how we arrived at our current social condition (why do we want what we want and do what we do, and what does it mean?) as well as where we are going. By becoming a little more familiar with the counter-narrative of sinful humanity, we can better understand the ambitions and desires that fuel modern thought, and we can more effectively resist the pervasive force of the cultural narrative.

Upon what basis does man apart from God rationalize his rage against Christian morality? Understanding the history and the development of Western thought can help us find our way. Knowing what the Bible has to say about where we are going, and why, will help us stand with courage, clarity and wisdom as the future unfolds and we seek to love Jesus with our whole hearts, minds and strength.

The Rise of the Anti-Christian Narrative

Much time, writing and analysis has been devoted to the subject of the development of what is known as the Western world view. It is beyond the scope of this book to provide a comprehensive look at the human journey, which began with seeking to understand the gods and developed into a crusade to shape individual destiny and morality. However, taking an introductory look at the history from the ancient world to the modern world can help us understand and prepare for what is to come.

The ancients saw reality as having originated from somewhere beyond human perception, from a transcendent source that was beyond human comprehension. Throughout the last millennium, however, the arc of Western thought has bent in a very different direction—from upward to inward, from the power of the gods over the affairs of men to the power and potential of man to govern and wield power for and from within himself.

Two critical eras shaped the development of the modern understanding about reality and human existence: the era of the Renaissance and the Reformation, and the Age of Enlightenment that followed. The Age of Enlightenment was the climax of a rational and intellectual shift from ancient mysticism that began with Greek philosophical thought. It was the ancient Greeks who had separated the nonmaterial, or the supernatural world, from the material, or natural world, giving priority to understanding man and the world in which he lived.

Renaissance and Reformation

The European Renaissance, sometimes also known as the Age of Discovery, is broadly considered to have taken place from the mid-1400s and through the 1600s, and it was characterized by an intellectual and cultural emphasis on exploring the world and the limits of human possibility. As European civilization emerged from the Dark Ages, it began to seem reasonable for people to move beyond understanding themselves and their world morally, rationally and scientifically, in order to conquer it and reshape it around themselves. The Renaissance was like a love affair between intellectuals and human dignity, energized by the seemingly unlimited potential for human achievement.

The Western world witnessed a rebirth of art, music, literature, philosophy and more—the "humanities"—along with an increase of wealth and stability. Study of the ancient classical works of the Greeks and Romans, which have to do more with worldly than religious matters, influenced everything. Taken as a whole, the Renaissance was a reaction to the prior period of the slow decline and fragmentation of Christendom; the power of the Catholic Church had ruled over most of the nations of Europe, often unquestioned and unchallenged, for a millennium. The excesses and corruption of the Church, and its dictatorial and often brutal responses to the challenges to her power had wearied the intellectual, philosophical and political world.

The Renaissance and the Protestant Reformation became the towering challenges to the Catholic Church's power, and they were made possible by the self-interest of kings and merchants. These men of power and wealth found, through the Renaissance in Italy and the Reformation in Germany, a way to govern and to do business apart from the interference of the Catholic Church. For centuries kings, nobles and landowners had been forced to bow before the might of the papacy. As papal power and authority over kings began to decline, something new began to arise. What followed made our world today the way it is.

The Italian Renaissance flourished in part because of economic and political upheavals that were happening across Europe. These enabled the patronage of new ideas, artistic endeavors and humanistic education that began to reshape the manner in which citizens thought of themselves and the world around them. The rise of new European powers in Spain, France and Germany, along with the Protestant Reformation in Northern Europe, prepared the way for new approaches to relationship between Church and state and the dynamics of how people in power wield that power for the common good. Initially, the debate of that era was, to varying degrees, *anti-Church*, because the vast political power, great corruption and opulent wealth of the Catholic Church and the manner in which it demanded the fealty of both European kings and commoners was a source of great angst.

Over time, the tone of the conversation became more generally *anti-church*, as the institution itself sparked conflict and trouble across the European continent, from the Crusades and the conflict with Islam, to the later brutal Spanish Inquisition, and finally to the devastating and ultimately meaningless Thirty Years' War in central Europe. Protestants and Catholics sparred relentlessly, and the mixture of church, politics and economics was both volatile and grueling.

In summary, the era marked a dramatic shift away from the foundations of Christian thought, as summarized by historian Dr. Glenn S. Sunshine in his book, *Why You Think the Way You Do*,

> The Renaissance called into question both the method that had been accepted for centuries for finding truth and the very goal of intellectual life. The Reformation broke the unity of the church, the anchor that had held the medieval world together, as Latin Christendom fragmented into many competing churches. The Wars of Religion led many to question whether religion was as central to society as had been believed. The New World raised questions about biblical history and reliability, as well as about the justice and morality of God. And Pyrrhonism [philosophic doubt, skepticism] was like an acid that corroded everything it touched, leaving in doubt the very possibility of knowing anything at all.[1]

Against the backdrop of decades of religious wars—Christian and Muslim, Protestant and Catholic—and centuries of a monolithic Church misusing power, the common man was exhausted, and the rationalist was given cultural permission and funding to ponder the meaning of it all. The influential voices of the day raged against the abuses of the Church, and the faith of the Church was diminished or discarded altogether in favor of a new push toward rationalism and humanistic achievement without interference from the seemingly power-hungry clergy who had exercised so much control over the masses. The entire Christian enterprise—papal power, superstitious thinking, corruption, bloodshed and power-hungry opportunism within various sectors of the Church—disintegrated. The rationalists and humanists across Europe had shifted from anti-Church to anti-church before eventually shifting to our present *anti-Christian* view of the world.

On the heels of the Thirty Years' War, the Age of Enlightenment arrived.

The Enlightenment

Enlightenment thought did not deny Jesus as much as it exalted human rationality in a new and profound way—a way that powerfully shaped the world we live in today. It did not initially reject Christianity or Christ Himself. It did, however, adjust the understanding people had of themselves and the world around them from a Jesus-centered one to a human-centered one. Practically, this meant that reality was limited to what humans and our five senses could discover and perceive.

At the forefront of this change was René Descartes, known as the father of modern philosophy, who famously wrote, *cogito, ergo sum* ("I think, therefore I am").[2] Descartes was a conservative Catholic who was seeking to build a logical construct that would answer the Pyrrhonic challenge to truth (named for the Greek skeptic Pyrrho, who attacked apparent certainties by applying logic). In doing so, Descartes helped to redefine the source of our understanding about the nature of reality. Whereas formerly the God of the Bible served as the source of our understanding, Descartes considered human knowledge to be a self-sufficient source of understanding.

Working from Descartes's ideas, Francis Bacon, often called the father of empiricism, established a standard of probability versus rational certainty. In doing so, he established a new framework for modern thinkers—the concept of cumulative progress and the idea that we can and should know more than those who came before us.[3] The idea that we should know more than our predecessors (and that things will therefore keep improving) had simply not occurred to thinkers prior to this.

The influence of Bacon's thought shaped the manner in which we as a society think and reason. It could be argued that he was singularly responsible for our scientific culture and its collaboration that promotes innovation and discovery. His scientific method of analysis and his vision for a scientifically oriented utopian future pushed the thinkers of his era to take significant steps toward an age of religious plurality and technological progress. Bacon took the promise and potential of man, awakened during the Italian Renaissance, and built significantly upon that foundation. He dreamed of a time when humanity, freed from the religious dogma and traditions that he felt stunted human progress, would be able to build a better world, one that would be united around scientific rationality, without prejudices and biases introduced by emotion.

How could Bacon have foreseen the unintended consequence of his utopian idealism? Today we live in a world that has replaced the religious dogma and tradition of a powerful, bureaucratic, international Church with scientific dogma; now we are steeped in pervasive academic traditions that are persistently loyal to a utopian ideal without religious interference. In Bacon's attempt to slay one giant, he accidentally replaced it with another of the same kind.

In light of the religious wars and devastation of the previous era, the work of Descartes, Bacon and later Sir Isaac Newton brought to birth a new optimism about human progress and future potential. Philosophers were seeking a more tolerant expression of faith, one that was less superstitious and more rational in its expression. By shifting the focal point of the universe from a transcendent God to humankind and the natural world, Enlightenment philosophers removed God from daily life and set Him at a distance from the affairs of human beings. This approach is called Deism, and it began to influence political, philosophical and scientific leaders.

Wanting to be free from the shackles of Catholic tradition and dogma, Enlightenment thinkers went beyond the Renaissance exploration of the beauty, dignity and capacities of humanity to declare that anything outside of human ability to think or perceive would therefore logically not exist. This would make a man the center of his own moral universe. For that reason, he would be able to determine the course of his own story.

Enlightenment philosophers, such as Voltaire, introduced ideas of human liberty that encouraged the Enlightenment critiques (and later attacks) against Catholic doctrine and practice, laying the foundations for modern conceptions about "tolerance." This enabled people to more freely voice their opposition or intolerance regarding ideas that they disagreed with. Voltaire promoted the toleration of opposing religious viewpoints and critiques as well as advocating for religious freedom and philosophical expression. However, in his rhetoric, which was directed toward the Christianized monarchies of Europe, it was clear that Voltaire himself wanted liberty to express his severe *intolerance* of the Catholic faith and practice. This served in part to inspire and inform the logical end and expression of his arguments—the bloody and terrifying French Revolution.

G. K. Chesterton summarized the consequence of Voltaire's ideas in his essay, "Anti-Religious Thought in the Eighteenth Century":

> Take the determining example of the Spanish Inquisition. The Spanish Inquisition was Spy Fever. It produced the sort of horrors such fevers produce; to some extent even in modern wars. The Spaniards had reconquered Spain from Islam with a glowing endurance and defiance as great as any virtue ever shown by man; but they had the darker side of such warfare; they were always struggling to deracinate a Jewish plot which they believed to be always selling them to the enemy. Of this dark tale of perverted patriotism the humanitarians knew nothing. All they knew was that the Inquisition was still going on. And suddenly the great Voltaire rose up and shattered it with a hammer of savage laughter. It may seem strange to compare Voltaire to a child. But it is true that though he was right in hating and destroying it, he never knew what it was that he had destroyed.[4]

What had Voltaire destroyed? Voltaire, like other Enlightenment voices in France, criticized both religious practitioners and religion itself; in pointing the finger at the untrustworthy religious authorities, he called into question the entire practice of religion. This led to a wholesale rejection of not only Catholic religious leadership, but also of Catholicism. The very foundations upon which France had been built were tossed aside during the French Revolution, whose principal leaders drew courage from Voltaire's very words in order to execute their bloody rejection of the Christian faith. With Voltaire came the raging need to reform nations *from* their Christianity, instead of seeing Christianity as a moral means to hold wicked men accountable.

The legacy of his wit and the sharpness of his critique live on in the modern zeal to secularize society and to deliver it from the "harmful" and "oppressive" influences of Christian thought.[5]

Like his rival and enemy, Voltaire, who despised and mocked him, Jean-Jacques Rousseau's ideas also contributed to the stirring of a national rage against the wealthy elite, the lavishly decadent monarchy and the greedy and corrupt Catholic Church. Rousseau wrote about the social contract that people have with one another and their responsibility to one another under the authority of the state, and his ideas laid the groundwork for modern concepts about government and socialism. Today's vilification of the rich and the moral justification of financial equality find roots in Rousseau's hatred of financial inequality and elitism. His ideas have matured into the modern Democratic-Socialist appeal, in which the ideal is the readjustment of wealth inequality as a part of a social justice crusade that has the result of dignifying covetousness and envy as virtues, rather than viewing them as vices.

Rousseau placed much faith in the democratic state to deliver men into a just distribution of wealth and thereby to produce good will in a population, yet the very forces he identified within the human heart that produce great envy and discontent are also at work within the governments he romanticized.

Baruch Spinoza, whose ideas were inspired by Rousseau's, should be understood as one of the most influential and important of the Enlightenment philosophers. His work powerfully altered the conversation among scholars and thinkers about the nature of God, in particular the manner in which we understand Him as a divine being. Spinoza's logic formulated a powerful attack against the concept of God as a Person who can be described in any human terms. To him, any depictions of God as a Father, a King or, specifically, as a Judge would be logical impossibilities. He believed that to conceive of God as a Judge is to introduce harmful and debilitating fears that enslave the human race and bind it to destructive hopes and superstitions.[6] Spinoza's importance must be understood in relationship to another key idea that he introduced: Whereas the framers of the U.S. Constitution advocated for a separation of Church and state, Spinoza advocated a century earlier for a removal of the church from the state.

Spinoza's reasoning stemmed from his desire for everyone to be free from fear. In his *Theological-Political Treatise*, Spinoza makes his arguments in favor of a state or commonwealth free of religious authority, religious intolerance and all suppression of intellectual or religious disagreement. He began those arguments by seeking to remove the idea of scriptural infallibility or divine inspiration. His goal was the removal of the heart of religion from the shackles of what he understood to be corrupted and untrustworthy biblical texts tampered with by later authors. He asserted that these biblical authors ascribed their work to Moses, the prophets and others while inserting their own dogmas and religious practices, and he argued that these dogmas and practices have since produced fear and anguish in the lives of the followers of Christ.

The Bible, in Spinoza's understanding, was no different from any other aspect of the natural world. Therefore, he felt it should be subject to the governance of men who were, by nature, free beings. In other words, Spinoza sought to remove the Bible as a written work filled with ideas to which people must come under submission. He was strongly in favor of subjecting the content of the Bible to human governance. (Side note: Spinoza's perspective helped Thomas Jefferson later feel comfortable excising the supernatural aspects of the biblical narrative from his personal Bible.) Once the Bible has been reduced to an ordinary book over which we can exercise our authority, we can simply remove or ignore the elements we do not like or agree with.

Into the Modern and Postmodern Era

These ideas are representative of the demanding questions that challenged first the authority of the Church in the Renaissance era, followed by the authority of the state in the Enlightenment era. These ideas and questions had significant ramifications not only for the Western understanding of what the world used to be like and of what had passed away but, more importantly, for the world that came to be established in post-Enlightenment, post-Industrial Revolution Europe.

Significant questions had been raised, including, How should a person come to governmental power, and by what right did some select people rule and govern the affairs of the rest of the people? Upon what basis did people grow in their strength and advantage, and could they improve their situation? If the Church had been wrong about, for example, the centrality of the earth in our solar system (in Galileo's time), then what else could the Church be wrong about? If the Church is wrong about a number of things, why should society be subject to it at all?

These questions led to a more haunting and potent question: If we remove the European powers and families that have ruled for centuries, what system of governance should we replace them with? How should society be organized? Who should determine the fate of populations of people and the natural world, and upon what basis are we going to make our moral and civil determinations? In summary: How do we know that we are right, and that our ideas should shape and govern civil society?

On an individual level, the change in one's sense about reality (from considering it to be transcendent and divine to viewing it as the result of inward perception and personal discovery) altered values and which things mattered. In due course, the Renaissance and the Enlightenment redefined success, the Western sense of purpose and achievement, as well as how citizens relate to authoritative power and those who wield it. The Industrial Revolution and the democratic societies that followed dramatically redistributed power from centralized religious and military institutions to economic and political entities. The redistribution of wealth and governance, added to the new humanism of the previous eras, transformed how people thought about themselves and the meaning of their lives.

With God no longer central as the defining source of human and societal purpose and the empowerment of people to define their own earthly path came a sense of meaninglessness, vanity and emptiness in the post-Industrial and postmodern era. At the same time, the base fears and ambitions of power-hungry people gave new life to old ideas through political debate. To the present day, the conflict between God, the church and society has been raging; the Enlightenment ideas that first challenged Christian thought are still alive and well.

Modern society has rejected the authority of the Church and has worked to remove its influence from the modern State. This has led to our current era of intensive effort to remove the *morality* of the Church and the Christian ethic, in order for society to achieve its more robust goals. On their face, these goals are intended to produce a just and fair society in which the weak, oppressed, disenfranchised and disadvantaged will at last be able to overcome current injustices. The underlying goals, however, include the removal of every superstitious, backward, harmful and destructive Christian ideal that hinders the progress of this just society that the various powers are seeking to build.

As we look to the past, we can see that moment in history in which Enlightenment ideas collided with a powerful Catholic Church in France. The end of that collision—the French Revolution, a revolt against the crown, the elite and the Church in France at the end of the eighteenth century—was violent, bloody and terrifying. (The bloodiest stretch was called the Reign of Terror, for good reason.) If we believe that in the days to come, power from heaven will accrue to the Church worldwide and that it will far surpass the power of the eighteenth-century Catholic Church (which I believe is part of the promise that the Bible declares) and if we are aware of a resurgence of Enlightenment ideas within the current cultural narrative, then here is the haunting question that we must wrestle with: What will the end look like for the Church in revival, as she operates with unprecedented power through the Holy Spirit? What happens when the Church with power collides with nations that have no interest in conceding power?

Another question that I am raising for consideration is this: If Enlightenment ideas fed a bloody overthrow of Catholic governance and national influence during the French Revolution, and those ideas still have life today, then how will the modern thought leaders, influenced by Voltaire and all the others, react to a global outpouring of the Holy Spirit?

The Anti-Christian Moment: the French Revolution

It has been argued over many years that the French Revolution was the natural outcome of the human-centered trajectory of thought supported by Rousseau, Voltaire, Spinoza and the

Enlightenment. What is still relatively unexplored is the question of how relevant are Enlightenment ideas today, and what the potential impact of those ideas could be within our modern religious context.

The French Revolution changed the social order in a way that was quite different from the way the American Revolution had changed it a few years earlier. The anti-Christian rage of the leaders of the French Revolution—the radical left-wing Jacobins and their leader Maximilien Robespierre—led to draconian and oppressive measures to de-Christianize nations and close churches. Even the Gregorian calendar was replaced for many years by the French republican calendar, which was designed to reflect a secularized society built on the foundations of reason as the premiere "guiding light" of society rather than the archaic foundations of religion and faith.

The Enlightenment marked the end of a very old world and feudal systems as well as the dawning of colonialism and the Industrial Revolution. It was the beginning of the rise of a very prosperous middle class in Europe—particularly in Britain and France—that marked the start of an era that would end very violently in 1914 because of World War I.

What can we say about this era of the development of modern thought—which led directly to the emergence of Napoleon and Hitler? These ideas undergird modern political, ideological and philosophical thought. Over the past two centuries, these ideas were the spark that ignited progress, unleashed historic wealth and improved the standard of living for millions of the citizens in many nations. Yet these same ideas led to monstrous acts of violence; the rise of nationalism and totalitarian, despotic rule; and colonialization, with its horrific oppression and exploitation of slaves, races and the resources of distant nations that bear deep scars to this day.

There is a logical end to the rationalistic, secularized and humanistic society that matured into a new expression during the Enlightenment. What is noteworthy for our context is the explosive spread of religion in our modern world. Whereas the political, military, media and cultural climate in the primary nations of the earth has been approaching a humanistic, anti-Christian apex toward which it began to climb in the late eighteenth century, the frame of mind in the middle class and the poor of the earth has been far more religious. Take, for example, the rapid spread of Spirit-filled, Pentecostal Christianity; Islam; and other religious forms and expressions. Even as the cultural revolutionaries of the 1960s proclaimed that God was dead, the Jesus people movement of the 1970s arose and churches grew dramatically.

One could argue that the Enlightenment only took hold with the elite and the powerful members of society, who served as a philosophical base to remove power from European royalty and distribute it to a new ruling class. The underlying themes and ideas from the Enlightenment informed this new ruling class regarding how to order society without God and how individuals could be truly free. Rousseau famously began his seminal book, *The Social Contract*, with the cry, "Man was born free, yet everywhere he is in chains." Rousseau and Voltaire, in their own diametrically opposed ways, raged against God, His Church and what they considered to be the oppressive abuses of power that accompanied religious expression.

However, the removal of Christianity from the new seats of power did not in fact remove oppression, injustice or wickedness. In France, then Russia, then Germany, it led to something else entirely. The question that our generation must face together is this: If Enlightenment ideas still fuel the new ruling class today, will the cycles of history repeat themselves one more time before the Lord returns? What will happen when Enlightenment-fueled secular powers collide with a revived, globally influential Church empowered by the Holy Spirit? From the resulting collision, could one final despotic power arise who will trouble the earth as Napoleon, Hitler and Stalin have before?

In the next chapter, we will shift from the impact of the developments of the eighteenth century to the world of today. We will examine the cultural narrative of our time and the demand that it places on the Western world to conform to its tenets. We also will take a look at two other important voices that have shaped our modern cultural narrative, Georg Hegel and Karl Marx. Their ideas about historical process and necessary revolution have powerfully influenced the postmodern, oppressive, shame-based social justice era in which we now live.

8

The Modern Expression
of the Cultural Narrative

When one examines the current social media scene with its influencers and content producers, its wish fulfillment and cheap performance art, its individualized world of curated posts and pervasive selfies, the gross amount of narcissistic self-adoration that is exploding out of our culture is breathtaking. In just a cursory glance at the social media world, you will quickly encounter our individualistic love affair with ourselves. It is paradoxically both shocking and predictable that this degree of self-love would appear side by side with a contrasting wave of loathing and contempt for others. I see the vitriol and hatred that is expressed online toward others on a daily basis as a powerful window into what Paul called "the mystery of lawlessness" (2 Thessalonians 2:7).

Something else has begun to unfold in social media—we now have the ability to destroy one another's lives and livelihood with just a few keystrokes. All that it takes is a mere accusation made public. Our online interconnectivity makes it possible for someone's world to be turned upside down through social pressure and deceptive (or truthful-but-merciless) messages. With even a single post, someone's reputation, social-professional relationships and career can all be destroyed.

Whether we realize it or not, this development too can be traced to the men of the Renaissance, and later the Enlightenment, through the Age of Revolution and into our modern world. Social media rage is the latest expression of the interior antagonism of many different voices over the centuries. The force of these many arguments and philosophical contributions has changed the way the people of the world react to one another.

We need to be able to see clearly what the world is like now and what this means for our children and their children. Otherwise, we will not be able to strengthen our interior life in Christ sufficiently to bear the weight of it. In my observation, this is where modern Christian positivism and fundamentalist negativism fail to engage in a productive dialogue. In the name of happiness and hope, Christian positivists ignore the actual state of things and the very real threats that are emerging; their unrelenting optimism causes others to stop taking the encouragers seriously and to look elsewhere for counsel and perspective. In the name of truth and discernment, Christian negativists sound a continual alarm and stir up fears about many possible harmful outcomes; their never-ending state of alarm causes others to stop taking their warnings seriously and to tune them out. The Church lacks a unified voice; it has become numb and sluggish—or fearful and reactionary.

The many, many options and voices we have to choose from in our digital world lead to endless noise, confusion and a kind of echo-chamber tribalism. We are not that different from the Western world as a whole as we drift toward tribalism, gravitating toward places of ideological comfort and safety. All the while, we keep stoking the anger and fear that is driving our world toward increased division and strife.

Ideas can and do have consequences, and the ideas that were born in reaction to a restrictive, powerful church organization in the Middle Ages—ideas that have empowered and given voice to anti-Christian thought and practice—have begun to blossom into maturity in our generation. We are, as a society, arriving at a destination that has taken five or six centuries to come to—a world without God, without Christians, without biblical morality and theology. Again, some Christians are skeptical that it is coming to this point, content to live their lives and engage the system that is becoming more and more hostile toward them, ignoring, for now, the increasing demand for cultural conformity. Others are aware, but they are fighting back with hearts filled with fear, anger, passion and zeal, rallying others to do the same. Where do you fall on the spectrum?

The Social Credit Score System

Recently, the Chinese government has launched a social credit score system. The aim is to promote the idea that "keeping trust is glorious and breaking that trust is disgraceful."[1] The system is similar to a private credit score. This, however, is a public reputation score. Through facial recognition systems, data analysis technology and viral reporting incentives, the Chinese government is able to regulate moral behavior that goes beyond criminal activity. Loud music, jaywalking or skipping dinner reservations count against a person, while charity work, donating blood or community service can improve the social score, which is publicly accessible. The trust score rates what kind of citizen you are and whether or not your behaviors align with Communist Party goals and values.

In other words, the Chinese government has found a new way to persecute the Christian Church, whose numbers have increased greatly within their nation over the past seventy years. Because direct oppression and persecution of Christians has not worked well, the new way forward connects economic and social incentives to a score and a blacklist that has already impeded the travel of 13 million Chinese citizens over the past few years.[2] Being blacklisted can hamper a person's ability to engage in buying and selling, to attend prestigious colleges and to have access to potential employment opportunities. Citizens have been encouraged to report one another, and failure to report can be in and of itself a means of lowering one's social credit score. Having a low social credit score can also have a negative potential impact on family members as well as friends and known associates.

The Chinese citizens that I have spoken with are sober about this social credit system, and the political leaders that I have spoken with here in the United States are alarmed. These are powerful economic and social incentives to conform to the Communist Party line, to betray friends and family and to deviate from overt Christian behaviors.

As I listen to people's justifiable alarm regarding the Chinese government's initiative, I cannot help but think about the informal social credit system that is taking root in the West. Our system is not being implemented by an oppressive, totalitarian regime. Our system is being implemented by the masses via social media, and it is ruthlessly effective. It began years ago, when Christian organizations or organizations that represented conservative morality would identify behaviors or ideas that they deemed harmful to the public good. Once identified, these organizations would call for boycotts, public apologies and other concessions to strong-arm corporations and public figures to ally themselves with Christian or conservative values.

Recently, however, the tables have swiftly and soundly turned. Social consciousness regarding issues of race, abuse, gender, sexuality and more has expanded, and a measure of moral authority has been given to those who have felt historically oppressed, mistreated or abused. Morality within our culture is being very swiftly redefined around universal truths that have unified agreement regardless of ideological background (for example, "Hatred is bad") along with blanket moral applications of those truths (for example, "Your words are hateful") and subsequent harsh penalties for breaches of moral conduct (for example, "No one should associate with you").

This is the grassroots, or democratized, Western version of the social credit system. In the East, the system is being applied and implemented through a despotic government, while in the West, the system is being applied and implemented through the social pressure from victims of varying forms of injustice. Both versions of the social credit system, along with the religious version that came before them, are at root despotic and controlling. This is the logical outcome of Rousseau's notions of liberty achieved through the social contract that we make with one another to achieve the common good. If God is removed from the equation and His Word is not part of the moral calculus of a righteous social order, then who decides and defines what the common good is?

The Anti-Christian Narrative

Since the Renaissance, as we have seen, the rage of men toward the constraints and dogmas of the Christian faith has gained strength and cultural influence. The burgeoning anger toward Catholicism during the Renaissance that boiled over into open hostility toward the Church and the Christian faith during the Enlightenment has progressed into more sophisticated iterations of anti-Christian thought. After the Enlightenment, the post-Christian era of philosophical thought began to emerge, from Napoleonic France to Victorian England. Philosophers, thinkers and scholars moved on from a Christian world view, neither working from it nor challenging it as such. Philosophical thought had moved into the realm of imagining the course of the world and human progress without God or religion or faith. With the shackles of Christian thought and dogma removed, just think of the possibilities!

The world as they knew it was filled with glorious new prospects because of the Industrial Revolution and colonial expansion. As wealth flowed into the nineteenth-century European powers, philosophers considered questions of human progress and the arc of human development. Freed from the narrative of Christian faith that predicted a specific end to the human journey, the philosophers of that era nevertheless needed to wrestle with difficult truths such as, "What does sudden, massive wealth expose regarding the human condition?" (Answer: They observed that corruption came with a sudden increase of wealth.)

The dark history of the exploitative colonialism of the powers of Europe is a vast subject that is beyond the scope of this discussion. Suffice it to say that the actions of the colonizers became a dark stain on what was understood to be a bright moment of possibility. Wars and conflicts occurred across Europe and the new United States of America; despotic rulers and weak monarchs passed away. The old world faded into memory and a new and modern world was slowly being born. What did this indicate? Despite the worst impulses of humanity, could civilization progress into something better, even a utopia?

Two men in particular made a significant impact on modern thought as they looked to address the true nature of man in relationship to the search for a utopian ideal: Georg Hegel and Karl Marx. Today's secular society owes much to the historical process that these men initiated.

Georg Hegel was a post-Enlightenment German philosopher in the early 1800s who understood history as a process by which, through philosophical collisions over time, society moves closer to universal truth, or reality. He defined the struggle to know and understand as a necessary conflict between opposing views—the thesis and the antithesis—by which we come to a better version of the two opposing ideas—the synthesis. Through debate and difficulty, the historical process progresses, moving closer and closer to actual truth and reality.

In his groundbreaking work, *The Phenomenology of Spirit*, Hegel presented the idea of the "World Spirit," the term he used to describe the collective consciousness of humankind and its necessary growth and development. Hegel believed that, over time, as society progresses and ideas collide and synthesize, new and better ideas emerge, and humanity progresses toward what he understood as the "Absolute Spirit," or the logical end point of the synthesis of ideas. For Hegel, the ideal state or utopia would be when synthesized truths would be capable of progressing from generation to generation. Then over time, the collective consciousness of humanity would reach an apex of absolute truth, after which progress would cease, having reached the climax of reason and truth. A society shaped by truths of that quality would, by definition, be perfect.

Nearly forty years later, a man named Karl Marx built on his work. Marx applied Hegel's ideas and methodologies to the political and economic arenas to address the increasing inequality between the rich and the poor in the new capitalist systems that were emerging from feudalism. He was not interested in philosophical synthesis leading to the truth; Marx was interested in class struggle and the revolutions necessary to displace and replace ruling powers. Marx's goal was for society to achieve a conflict-free state by means of redistributing power. His theory of the liberation of society involved transferring power from the smaller ruling class to the much larger proletariat, or general members of society.

This conflict-free utopian ideal could not be attained, of course, as long as Christianity was in the way. Marx opposed Christianity, Christian morality and religion in general, seeing them as part of the superstructures used by the ruling classes to acquire and maintain their power. Vladimir Lenin and Joseph Stalin later instituted Marx's ideas in Communist Russia after the Russian Revolution, and this was followed by Mao Tse-tung's Chinese Communist revolution.

In the 1950s and '60s, Marxist philosophy began to expand beyond the political and economic spheres into the realm of theology. Liberation theology began to emerge within the Catholic Church as a means of shifting the attention of the Church to the plight of the poor in oppressed situations. Liberation theology advocated the restructuring and reorganizing of the Church to give preferential attention to those who were "insignificant," "marginalized," "unimportant," "needy," "despised" or "defenseless."[3]

More recently, Marxist philosophy and concepts have expanded into social and moral arenas of thought and study. A few analysts have coined the controversial term, "cultural Marxism,"[4] the roots of which can be traced back to Antonio Gramsci of Italy and Georg Lukacs of Hungary, who viewed the failure of Marxism after World War I as a product of the superstructures that were holding back the necessary revolution and societal changes. They felt that it was the superstructures connected to Western values, specifically both American individualism and Christianity, that were hindering societal change. They thought that Christian morality formed immoveable planks that stood in the way of societal evolution, and therefore Christian morality must be attacked in order to remove its societal influence.

From their writings and influence, German Marxists formed the Frankfurt School of Critical Theory in 1923 to advance the theory as a means of destabilizing the cultural superstructures hindering societal change. Critical theory is a means of criticizing the way a culture and society as a whole function in order to bring change.[5] One of the members of the Frankfurt School, Herbert Marcuse, came to America and began advancing the idea that a Marxist revolution would happen by means of the raising up of oppressed or marginalized groups—some of the very groups identified in Latin America by liberation theologians. Marcuse was one of the early proponents of the left-wing view of tolerance.[6]

The current iteration of Marxism (cultural Marxism) is not what critics oppose in and of itself. What is objectionable to some critics is the idea that a few Marxist scholars could have such an outsized impact on modern progressive thought. To them, the idea sounds conspiratorial and exaggerated.

I am not advocating the idea that our current social and moral condition is the fruit of a widespread Marxist conspiracy nor am I attributing the current cultural narrative to a handful of philosophers and professors. There is a much more powerful and insidious conspiracy at work, and the root system runs much deeper than that of Marxist thinkers and writers. These people, and thousands like them, gravitate toward and then propagate these kinds of ideas and ideologies because of the deeper conspiracy that operates imperceptibly in the heart of fallen humankind. The mystery of lawlessness, the rage of the nations and the anti-Christian longing that churns like a storm in the souls of prideful, broken, unrighteous people have always inspired the rhetoric of freedom and liberty. In today's language, we have "tolerance and justice."

The social, moral and economic controls that accompany the calls for liberation, tolerance and freedom therefore always lead to despotic or totalitarian ends. This is the nature of the human heart at war within itself, struggling between fallenness and the conscience, which leads to wars against those around us. By nature we are "children of wrath" (Ephesians 2:3).

The course of this world flows according to the dictates of the prince of the power of the air, the spirit who now works in the sons of disobedience (see Ephesians 2:2). Therefore, our lives apart from God are driven by lust, not love. (Lust in this context means the interior longing and self-seeking agendas that drive our actions and behaviors.) It is our own self-seeking agenda that causes us to befriend the world and to seek to conform it into our image rather than praying and contending for Jesus to conform it to His. Lust drives us to build the world that we want, according to the moral code and rules that we prefer (see 1 John 2:15–17). The collective good and that which best serves the social order is then defined as "those who are in agreement with me." Christians will be unyielding in a Marxist construct because Marxists will not conform even to a democratically driven consensus defining the collective good, whereas Christians must continually yield to the leadership and authority of Christ.

The Christian's continual insistence on yielding to a divine authority (an authority that the lost have a deep inward longing to overthrow and remove) is what makes the Christian someone who the world must either force to conform—or remove altogether. As long as Christians are uncompromising regarding the cross, Jesus and how He defines love and truth, there is no place for them in this world as it has been currently constructed.

The world has arrived at a tragic and treacherous destination. We have not yet arrived at the destination that the Bible describes as the "days to come." What we have seen up to this point was described by Jesus as wheat and tares that grow together (see Matthew 13:24–30). But it may be more apt to describe our current situation as being like two very different powder kegs that are being set up to detonate dramatically in the future.

On the redemptive side, the Kingdom of God has been steadily growing and expanding over the centuries. In recent years, as we have seen, the pieces are slowly being moved in place for the Lord's endgame to bring justice to the world and His Son back to the planet. Global prayer, multiplied missions, and developments in Israel and Jerusalem are all setting the stage for an explosive revival that will shake the earth.

On the other side, the prince of the power of the air and the sons of disobedience that he has been working through have set things in motion toward a very different desired end. That end is either the conformity of Christianity to the current cultural narrative—or the removal of Christianity from the world scene. The tension is high, as the fundamentals of Western culture that have been derived from its Judeo-Christian history seem to have become intolerable to the toleration-and-justice movement that operates from a Marxist base.

From a Marxist perspective, the pillars of Western capitalistic ("oppressive") society are superstructures of Christian thought that work against the necessary revolution to overturn corrupt and exploitative governments and powers. Historically, this has been why radically left-wing voices have raged against the "intolerance" of the Christian world view, calling for tolerance. Yet paradoxically, these same voices have denounced belief systems within Christianity as intolerable. (Within a Marxist system, these belief systems need to be removed to make a way for necessary societal transformation to take place.)

In our day, there is no widespread global persecution of Christianity with the aim of its removal because there still seems to be the hope that its adherents can either be bullied into silence, shamed into irrelevance or seduced into conformity. The current wave of Democratic Socialists do not agree with the underlying principle of Marxism that says that societal transformation can only come through revolution and conflict. They hold the belief that, with the moral high ground secured, their ideas can eventually win the day. As we have seen within our own societal context, they are seeking the removal of the superstructures through political and ideological means, seeking power to legislate the necessary change while simultaneously applying cultural pressure. Up to this point, the pathway to change has been slow, deliberate and incremental.

However, when worldwide revival ignites the Kingdom of God, it will turn the kindling into an explosion. This will be the catalyst that will push the nations from seduction into rage, hatred and persecution. Historically, the revived Church always becomes (according to awakened consciences) an unreasonable Church. Two examples: After the First Great Awakening, the American colonies could no longer in good conscience continue to fund the wars and lavish lifestyle of King George III. When the issue of conscience touched the issues of finance and taxation, neither side would budge, because of the economics of the situation. This sparked war. Then after the Second Great

Awakening stirred the consciences of the Northern U.S. states regarding slavery, sparking the holiness and abolition movements, the U.S. Southern states saw a threat to their thriving economy, which had been built on slavery.

In other words, there are always very intense social, moral, political and economic ramifications to a powerful revival, all the more when the revival is a global one. The awakened conscience of a unified, worldwide Church is a terrifying prospect for the wicked and oppressive powers of the earth to reckon with. A revived Church cannot be seduced, bargained with, intimidated or silenced, and it will possess newly acquired divine power to oppose the destructive and immoral course that the nations of the earth have embarked upon. The governments and corporations of the nations of the earth all have much to lose if a revived and powerful Church is able to reassert her will regarding societal change. A Joel 2 revival of the Church will leave the nations at a crossroads regarding the future. There can be no peaceful coexistence with a Church that is unified, revived and filled with the power and authority of the Holy Spirit.

Lovers of Self, Money and Pleasure

Through his letter to Timothy, Paul gave one of his final warnings to the Church, presenting a clear and detailed picture of the course the world is taking. He defines the source of the problems in the "perilous times" to come: the human lusts that drive sinful behaviors. That is to say, behind all of the rage, the arguments and debates, the agendas and the intimidation, lies the love of self and the love of money (see 2 Timothy 3:1–5). These are the lusts that produce all of the self-promoting, blasphemous opportunism. When people exhibit a lack of loyalty to anything except their own empire-building, they also lack love, reverence, forgiveness, trust, self-control and true kindness. This is what drives the powers and rulers who are building a world without God and His morality. They make themselves their own highest authority, refusing to answer to a higher authority, and they abandon the restraints of biblical morality and Christian influence. The removal of the Christian superstructure is causing the world to descend into madness, with every man living for himself and for his own good, fighting to conform the world around him to his own ends.

The "form of godliness" that Paul speaks of is part of the self-centered pragmatism that takes advantage of any means to the end of personal power. If religion can be useful to convince the masses to move forward, if it fits or complements the cultural narrative that serves that end, then a place will be made for it. If religion is not useful to the self-centered end goals, it can easily be discarded, along with church associations, relationships and anything else that impedes "progress."

Yes, as Paul wrote, this world is a perilous, dangerous place for Christians. However, we do not need to fear either the world as it is nor where it is headed. We do not need to retreat, hide or draw back in any way. The Scriptures are clear about the course of this world and its future apart from God. And the Scriptures are clear about the victory and glory of the Church in the days to come.

We who are the Church do not need to worry about the future. The Father is going to place a mature, beautiful, powerful Church on display for all the nations to see. When they see God's character reflected in His Bride, many will repent and abandon the course the world has set, turning toward the passionate love of the Son of God.

Moving forward with a clear understanding of both the darkness around us and the light to come, we do not need to prepare our hearts and lives to merely endure and survive the ravages of the world around us. Instead, we can prepare our hearts and lives to thrive when the darkness is greatest, to be the most hopeful when things seem the most bleak, and to be loving and merciful toward our enemies when they rage toward us with hatred.

How can we do this? How can we prepare to engage the world with that kind of love in the days to come? How can we keep standing, without offense, when those around us betray us, grow cold and turn away? In the next section, I will show you what God has promised to provide for His own.

PART THREE

THE PROMISE OF THE VICTORIOUS CHURCH

9

The Way of Victory and Redemption

The Scriptures give us the gift of perspective about the future. Scriptural perspective gives us the ability to walk forward with confidence in God's sovereign leadership, rather than quavering under intimidation.

A wise perspective makes it possible for us to prioritize—with sober-minded urgency in light of the hour in which we live—the things that really matter. Scripture is telling us where things are going so that we can be alert and ready for what is coming. As we have been exploring in this book, it is the Father's plan to turn even the rage of the nations to work for our good, using the furnace of severe trials to produce deep love, loyalty and maturity within the hearts of His people. God is able to make *all* things work together for our good, even the most extreme circumstances and pressures (see Romans 8:28). He turns pressure to our advantage, working within us greater measures of perseverance and steadfastness. He works a radical transformation in our hearts and gives us great hope for the future as we see His handiwork (see Romans 5:1–5).

God's grand plan to provide an eternal companion for His Son is the very premise of His creation (see Ephesians 5:31–32; Revelation 19:7–9). Everything that God did in creation and all He continues to do throughout history is serving His plan to prepare a Bride for His worthy Son. Therefore, the essential centerpiece of our story is not the coming trouble. Rather, it is God's glorious master plan to use Satan's own rage against him, to allow the rage of the nations to help perfect a beautiful, mature, powerful Bride who is worthy of ruling the nations of the earth alongside her Bridegroom, Jesus.

By the grace of God, together we are *becoming something*. His wisdom and perfect leadership waste nothing. He labors with jealous love to prepare a glorious Bride—meaning those individual believers who have combined their lives within the Church—a seasoned, tested and mature people who love deeply with unshakable loyalty and authority.

The Way of Urgency

How then do you and I move forward as individuals to partner with what the Lord is doing? By now, I hope that you have already begun to lay hold of one of the most critical aspects of preparation for the future: a sense of urgency that comes by grace, through what Paul called a "spirit of wisdom and revelation in the knowledge of Him" (Ephesians 1:17).

A spirit of revelation is the proverbial light bulb turning on in your mind, when suddenly something you have never understood just makes sense. This moment of clarity-via-grace is often followed by a measure of conviction to help you respond to what you have come to understand.

Daily, you and I are stuck in a dark room, unable to see until God turns the light on. In His kindness, the Lord wants to stir up our hunger and holy curiosity to seek Him so that we can know Him better. We respond to the divine invitation to seek His face by making room in our schedule for Him. We give Him our attention because we want to, and the rewards are great.

As we set aside regular and frequent times to read His Word, talk to Him and listen for His responses (expressed to us in our thoughts, emotions and desires), He gives us more grace. This is the beauty of God's leadership: He starts the conversation with us, helps us find joy in it and then responds to our responses to Him during the conversation. Through it all, we come to know and love Him more and more.

As I have noted, I am not the most impressive Christian, nor am I the most anointed intercessor or prophet. I find my daily life to be quite normal and unimpressive, and in my prayer life, I am always asking God for help regarding my character and my responses of love toward Him and others. I have much growth ahead of me, and He knows that. More uncomfortably, He is also aware of the hidden motives of my heart that drive my behaviors. Yet, to my unending joy, He loves me with wholehearted commitment and a burning, holy jealousy.

He never quits; He never tires; He never stops. And He refuses to allow me to settle for where I am at today. Joyfully, He continues to fight for me and to connect me with His vast and endless love. This gives me courage to reach back to Him, even when I feel thoroughly inadequate and flawed. Then I am reminded of what I have learned from His Word: the fact that He is never scandalized or offended by my inadequacies and flaws. He knew what He was signing up for when He called me those many years ago. He knew the mess that I was in then, and He knew the mess that He would still be delivering me from today. Even still, He wanted me, and He has stayed with me. I draw much encouragement from seeing the areas of real maturing—clear evidence of His handiwork in my life.

The reason that it is important to take time to remind ourselves of these truths—particularly now, in a book like this—is that we often and easily compartmentalize truths from the Bible. Even while we are developing a sense of the urgency of the times we are living in, we must remember His abiding love. The Father loves us so deeply. Every time we spend time reading His Word or praying, we grow a little more in intimacy with Him.

His message of loving intimacy needs to be a dynamic part of our understanding of the urgency of the times and seasons in which we live.[1] How else can we watch faithfully and pray fearlessly regarding the timing of His return? When Christians find out that they are supposed to be living with a sense of urgency, watching and praying about the timing of Jesus' return, they tend to fixate on these new (to them) truths and forget about staying connected to an ever-loving God in a dynamic relationship.

Never forget how much you need Him here and now as well as in the events of the unknown future. The scriptural truth that is front and center in my own life is the truth about my ongoing need for Jesus' help. I need Him. Apart from Him, I can do *nothing*. Therefore, I make sure that I am abiding in the vine (see John 15:5), and I exert myself in an effort to stay connected with Him through loving obedience to His commands. The glory of abiding in Him is that my need for help—which is an introductory sort of urgency—pushes me to seek Him out continually. Over time, as I stay with it and continue to behold

Him and walk with Him, a true desire for Him gets added to my need for Him.

In other words, I start out needing Jesus, and over time, I also *want* to be with Him. In the beginning, my relationship with Him is immature, self-centered and self-protecting—mostly functional in nature. His grace is serving a necessary purpose in my life. Astonishingly, He knows this, and it does not put Him off. He patiently pursues the process of thawing my cold, self-absorbed heart. As He thaws my heart, my relationship with Him changes. Instead of being merely functional, it becomes deeply personal. Jesus moves from being my source and supply to becoming my truest and dearest friend.

My sense of biblical urgency has changed and grown over time, as well. It began with my sense of need for God's help for the immediate concerns of daily life. (I prayed often in high school for help on exams!) I look back now and smile at the pettiness of my prayer requests, but from the Lord's perspective, the urgency worked. It got me into the conversation with Him. He never once turned me away when I asked Him for things, and in time He helped me shift my requests so that they would be based on His Word. I asked Him to help me understand His Word, and He did. Over time, as I matured in both my perspective and my prayer life, biblical urgency began to alert me to the scope and scale of my need for help.

When we begin to grasp the severity and the intensity—not to mention the glory and the power—of the days ahead, we come to Jesus with new resolve and an awakened sense of responsibility. We find that a life of intimacy fueled by urgency will accelerate our transformation into faithful servants of the King. Our priorities change. As we become awakened by grace to the urgent importance of the hour we are living in, our concern for those around us (awakened by Jesus as well) compels

183

us lovingly to serve, instruct, alert and equip others. We carry a vision for the maturity and enduring strength of those we love. We want them to be equipped to stay the course all the way to a victorious end.

We will treat discipleship differently when we see ourselves as part of a war and when we prepare ourselves for spiritual battles, both near and distant. Under the guiding hand of Jesus as our Shepherd and Leader, we are preparing ourselves and others to face tomorrow confidently.

The Way of Preparation

What does it actually look like for the nations to rage against God, and where is this going in the future? To help us gain a more concrete sense of where we need to grow and receive help from the Lord, let's take another look at His words:

> "Then they will deliver you up to tribulation and kill you, and you will be hated by all nations for My name's sake. And then many will be offended, will betray one another, and will hate one another. Then many false prophets will rise up and deceive many. And because lawlessness will abound, the love of many will grow cold. But he who endures to the end shall be saved. And this gospel of the kingdom will be preached in all the world as a witness to all the nations, and then the end will come."
>
> Matthew 24:9–14

Deception and oppression characterize the way Western culture expresses its rage against God and His people. Both are relational—and harmful—involving seduction and intimidation, and they serve the goals of either transforming Christianity into a watered-down morality that aligns with societal values or removing Christianity altogether. This is what we are facing on a daily basis. How can we as Christians balance the tensions between loving others with Jesus' love even as we confront the error and aggression around us? Wise spiritual preparation involves three ongoing aspects: a deep confidence in the Word of God, a life of active intimacy with Jesus and a growing responsiveness to the guidance and help of the Holy Spirit. By grace, these three things will provide us with the wisdom and clarity to know how to respond to the challenges posed by an anti-God world with both graciousness and clear-headed boldness.

I have found over the years that my love and compassion for broken and hurting people cannot exceed my love and passion for Jesus. I never want to put myself above Him, somehow thinking of myself as more loving and compassionate than He is. I never want to give more of my love and loyalty to other people than I do to Jesus Himself, because doing that—and perhaps all of us need to learn this the hard way—sets us up to oppose His leadership.

By remaining humbly dependent on the Spirit of God every day, my love and compassion for other people will flow out of my love and passion for Jesus. My life will be defined by His love. I will continue to reach out toward my ultimate goal, which is to love Jesus with all of my heart, soul, mind and strength (see Matthew 22:36–40). This is Jesus' greatest commandment and it is what life is all about.

Oh, the simplicity, power and glory of it all—love from Jesus brings love for Jesus, then love for others. For each one of us, our journey of growing in Christ is all about love, growing in His love and learning to give it away.

Amazingly, with all of the cosmic and global truths we find in Scripture, pure love is the most real of all. In the midst of so much surging rage and rejection and violence, I can know that He loves me. He loves *me*. He loves *you*. Therefore we love Him, and we follow Him wherever He leads.

From that simple place of love and affection from and for Christ, I am learning to love, to serve and to bless. As He becomes my dearest Friend, I learn to be a friend. This brings beauty into the midst of the madness. This is the glory of the Church in the midst of the storms.

I think that the reason that I get so vexed at times by modern Western Christianity is that I find the Bride so beautiful and worth fighting for, and I want the glory of this truth to permeate the life of every believer in Jesus. This has nothing to do with professional success, the numeric growth of congregations, personal recognition or influence. Our beloved Jesus had none of those things in His earthly life. Yet the Western Church seems to have been overinfluenced by modern culture (along with our human pride) to the point that it equates fruitfulness with "big" and "more."

The glory of Christianity is its simplicity. Its beauty lies in its hiddenness, not in renown or acclaim. For Jesus, it was all about loving His Father with His whole heart in the midst of the scorn and the rejection. Even His disciples represented varying degrees of foolishness, ranging all the way to outright corruption. Yet He loved them equally.

Through everything, we have to get back to the sweetness and simplicity of "me and Jesus." Whether you feel lost in the midst of the multitudes or alone on the mountaintop of success, you can treasure a quiet connection with Him. Even if you are important in the world's eyes, you must remain small and simple in your heart. Regardless of what you believe the future holds, nothing matters as much as your relationship with Jesus. Jesus is the constant. He is your anchor in the storm and your light in the darkness.

No storm is bigger or stronger than He is. With Him, you can bravely face the hurricane-force winds that are coming. The more real your secret life of loving Jesus becomes, the more precious and beautiful you will find it to be, and the more prepared you will be to "go there" when the rains come and the nations rage. You will have your dearest Friend to cling to, and He will show you what to do. Set your entire hope on Him today, so you will be ready.

The Way of the Heart

In Matthew 24–25, Jesus taught about the end of the age and His return, and then, before describing the final judgment, He applied His teaching in three parables to those He called to leadership.

I want to focus on the second parable (see Matthew 25:1–13), in which Jesus presented the idea that the delay related to His return would be longer than expected. This parable, the Parable of the Wise and Foolish Virgins, emphasizes prayer and growing our interior life in the Holy Spirit as we cultivate intimacy with Jesus. The heart of the parable is a warning to value wise decisions over foolish ones, because the time is coming when it will be too late to make up for bad decisions. The foolish people in this parable neglect to maintain their intimacy with God and are therefore unprepared to partner with the Bridegroom, Jesus.

Jesus' main exhortation to the Church regarding preparation for the future is to "watch," or to develop a vital heart connection with the Spirit.[2] In the Parable of the Wise and Foolish

Virgins, the primary idea is to prepare for the coming of the Bridegroom by buying oil. In that day, oil was used as fuel for lamps, as a food and as a medicine to heal sickness. Metaphorically, the oil represents the presence of the Spirit and our reach to connect with Him in prayer as we cultivate our secret life in God.[3] In this passage, Jesus is using the idea of lamps and oil to inform His audience of the need to prioritize light in a time of darkness and confusion. The oil, or the power and life of the Holy Spirit, fuels the lamp, which represents our ministry to others.

The proverbial oil of the Holy Spirit within us touches our hearts in different ways. It makes our hearts tender, enabling us to feel more of God's desire for us. This is critical as we combine the Word of God with our daily prayers. As we pray and read Scripture, the Holy Spirit works within us so that we experience the truth of what we are seeking to comprehend. Thus, active intimacy with Jesus causes us to grow, by grace, in our experiential knowledge. His truths are living and active within us, transforming and sensitizing us to the presence of the Lord.

This is beautifully simple, but what does it practically look like? In my case, I feel gratitude when I read truths about Jesus and His love. I cry as my heart is moved by His costly sacrifice and His willingness to fight for me. I am awestruck when I realize that my small, weak love moves and delights His heart. I want to grow in tenderness so that I am not dull or cold to His wonderful truths, but rather continually moved by them. The oil of the Holy Spirit's activity in my life increases my desire for Him as, repeatedly, I encounter His desire for me. An active life of engaging with the Holy Spirit illuminates my understanding. I gain new revelations of God's beauty. As I receive grace from the Word to see Jesus in new ways, I begin to receive corresponding grace to love what I see.

Early on in our walk of faith, the expressions of the guiding love of Jesus are not always attractive to us. The idea of becoming meek, lowly of heart and like a servant (becoming small to be great) or living before Him as an audience of One—none of it appeals to our prideful desire to attract attention to ourselves. We prefer to be heard, to get our own way and to have others acknowledge our excellence and our gifting. Jesus' Spirit shows us the Father as He is, which for some of us becomes our point of rejection. Confused by His wrath, troubled by His judgments and perplexed by His standards and laws, we either try to make God conform to our conceptions, or we reject Him altogether and go off to blaze our own trail through life. He does not become beautiful to the ones who do that.

But if the Spirit makes the Word attractive to us, we repent and receive God's wisdom—on His terms. Over time, that wisdom, which is His heart, becomes beautiful to us. His ways become lovely as we begin to love His leadership and His law, not only His benefits.

This works to impart to us the next benefit of the oil of the Spirit's activity in our heart and life: a zeal for righteousness, which helps us in our struggle with besetting sins. The spiritually bored Christian is in great danger of much compromise. Only by being fascinated with the beauty of Christ, along with having a tender heart moved by love and mercy, can we keep from sinning (and keep repenting when we do sin). When we follow the first commandment to love Jesus with our whole heart, then one of our primary rewards will be a joyful desire for holiness. Duty and shame will be replaced with delight. Our earnest pursuit of God will lead to the reward of more God. He Himself awakens our hearts to the desire for Him.

As we put our cold hearts before His, we gain a genuine zeal for righteousness wrapped in humility and gratitude. This is far from a self-righteous sense of superiority toward those around us who "don't get it" or are not like us. This zeal for righteousness fuels our compassion for the hurting and the broken. We want them to know the love of Jesus in the same way that we know it, and we want to remove the obstacles that keep them away from that love. We do not want to fix hurting and broken people so that they can be like us in their demeanor or lifestyle, but rather simply so that the hurting and the broken can come to know and to be like Jesus.

As the parable continues, the foolish virgins take their lamps (ministry) to engage with what the Bridegroom (Jesus) is doing, but they took no oil with them for the journey. In other words, they pursued their ministry or their occupation as their highest priority, forgetting about getting oil (pursuing their own relationship with Jesus). They valued their job, assignment or daily task more than obtaining the oil. And what happened? They were excluded from the wedding feast. The wise virgins, who did go out and look for oil first, were fully prepared for the feast, and they were admitted with joy. These are the ones who pursued the life and activity of the Spirit in their lives. They could proceed to the wedding feast confidently.

Our relationship with Jesus should be the most important thing in the world to us, higher than our assignments in ministry or our secular jobs. And if we are wise, we will be aware of our limitations and we will clearly acknowledge that our spiritual history in God and our spiritual preparedness cannot be transferred to others. (Just as the wise virgins could not simply hand over to the unwise virgins some of the lamp oil that they had purchased.) We need to seek God for ourselves, before we ever reach out in any kind of ministry, always remembering that God's grace cannot be earned; we can only position ourselves to receive it by giving of ourselves in costly obedience.

Our preparation of heart becomes a firm foundation under our feet that enables us to stand with great steadfastness and spiritual vitality in the face of great waves of cultural seduction and deception. This journey (allowing the Holy Spirit, through the Word of God and prayer, to transform our hearts and minds) takes us to the goal of complete agreement with the Lord, responsive to His leadership in obedience and love.

Nobody—including you and I—thinks of himself or herself as being deceived or aims to induce others to accept faulty world views and values. Each of us believes what we believe because we have found that over time those beliefs "hold up" and work for us. We are rarely able to self-assess our goals and desires to see if they truly align with the Word and the heart of Jesus. (Note: This is why pastors and pastoral leadership are so critical in our lives.) Equipped only with our flawed goals and broken, sinful desires, we are not capable of discerning any underlying distorted or unbiblical beliefs that we may harbor.

The desired end of heart transformation is so that we can stand under pressure, in the face of deception—not so that we can be dogmatic and combative or focused on winning arguments. I so often see an argumentative, "gotcha" culture within the Body of Christ. This goes beyond pulling down strongholds and arguments against the Lord (see 2 Corinthians 10:4–5). It hinders love to merely win arguments and, in the process, to assault the dignity of the person that we are arguing with. I am troubled by the way so many of us dehumanize the people who disagree with us. I see it as evil, even demonic, the way in which each side of a debate writes the other side off, questioning motives and associations, seeking to silence the opposition.

It is possible, you know, to be bold in our quest for truth from the Scriptures while still loving those who challenge us in apparent enmity.

After all, our battle is not "against flesh and blood, but against principalities, against powers, against the rulers of the darkness of this age, against spiritual hosts of wickedness in the heavenly places" (Ephesians 6:12). As part of the Church, we are not at war with the human race, but like Jesus, we long to see humanity saved and filled with the love and glory of Christ. We want revival, repentance and a massive turning of human hearts to Jesus by grace and the power of the Holy Spirit so that the air will be clear and the demonic influences will be removed. Then accusation will at last be silenced, and people will find it easier to hear and experience the life of Jesus. When we prepare our hearts through transformation by the Spirit (or "buy oil"), we position ourselves to respond in whatever way is appropriate to the situation. We can stand and be silent when necessary, stand and prophesy when prompted, or stand and serve while our enemies rage and vent.

In other words, if you and I are going to be capable of responding differently to the rage of the nations, we need to *be* different. It is one thing to write about revival; I need a personal revival on the inside that shifts my heart dramatically and that changes my default responses to pressure and accusation. Only then can I move easily with the Spirit rather than stumbling in compromise, reacting in anger and offense, or self-righteously shaming those who stand against the truth of the Word. I want to express the truth saturated with love and humility far more than I want to win arguments and humiliate others. I never want the knowledge of God to make *me* strong; rather I want it to accentuate His strength in my weakness as I love and serve others.

The Way of the Cross

We have learned that the way of victory and redemption is the way of heart preparation and transformation. A heart transformed is our best weapon against the loveless, brutal, self-seeking culture that is only going to intensify in the days ahead.

As the culture has become more self-centered, the broken and the hurting now seem to be making their brokenness and hurt central to their identity in their struggle against an unjust world. They will not find justice by going on that way. The current cultural "gospel" speaks of toleration and the suspension of oppressive ideologies, along with the cessation of practices and policies that cause pain. To do anything less is deemed "hateful," which in turn makes the "hater" deserving of intolerance, marginalization and second-class status. Then victims, ignoring the brokenness and injustice within their own souls, become the ones who define justice. Thus, they are blind to their own capacity to become oppressors.

The only way to break this cycle of injustice is to introduce both the oppressed and the oppressors to Christ. How did Jesus break the cycle of injustice? He went to the cross. His Bride will, in the days ahead, volunteer to take the same journey. We are not being called to prepare only for a future in which the Church suffers persecution and pain; the call to the cross for the Church begins here and now. Jesus, as the second Person of the Trinity who possessed all power, willingly submitted Himself to be oppressed and victimized. He chose to die for His haters in order to save and transform them. The great calling of the Church is to walk the same road, to model for a broken world a gospel response to oppression and hatred.

I see a narcissism-fueled, anti-Christian, dark and evil age that is beginning to crash in around us. However, this was true in Paul's day as well.[4] The answer in his day is the same answer for our day—which he prophesied about long ago. While we can arm ourselves with the information we need to crush the opposition and win the fight, that is not the way to go. Jesus could have done that and more. Yet He chose to be crushed for the sake of love. The preparation of our hearts for the present and future rage is not so that the modern Church can prevail in all of the arguments. We are preparing our hearts to go willingly and lovingly to the cross. For the sake of the world that rages and the people who despise and seek to oppress and marginalize us, our only rational biblical answer is the cross.

We would love to win in the game of King of the Hill. But the only way to win is to die to ourselves first. In this day and age, we are privileged to show the world who Jesus really is by taking the same journey in lowliness and humility that He took. To the world, this journey is an utter waste. However, from heaven's perspective it is a very beautiful journey that is near and dear to the Father's heart. Listen! I can hear the Spirit beckoning us onward, nearer to the cross. The world is waiting for us.

10

Preparing
the Next Generation

As you read this book, I pray that you are feeling stirred with a sense of personal responsibility. I hope that you are finding a fresh desire to prepare your own heart, and then to reach out to help others understand the times we are living in.

In light of where the world is heading, how can we be sure that we are handing the next generation a faith that endures? How can we build up our faith and our lives to walk victoriously through the storm, and bring our families along with us on the journey?

The study of the emotions of God and how He feels about His people is one of the most effective ways to connect our hearts to a dynamic life of devotion to Jesus. It touches on one of the deepest desires of the human heart: the longing for nearness to God, without shame. Every heart longs for this assurance. Yes, it is wonderful to know "God so loved the world that He gave His only begotten Son" (John 3:16), but we long for the assurance that God enjoys us as well. We want to know, "How does God feel about me?"

"I believe that God *loves* me," I have heard many times from young people, who then add tentatively, "But does He *like* me?"

Love and *like* are not quite the same, are they? Every Christian wants to know something that is fundamental to their spiritual growth. They have learned that God loves them because He *has* to. Love is who He is and what He does. They understand that, to a measure, His love has nothing to do with them. God loves because He loves, not because we are lovable, right?

They have learned the truth, yet it is not completed in their hearts. They know that love means unconditional forgiveness when they sin or make a mistake. It means that Someone paid the sacrificial price for them to go free. This good news stirred them to respond to the grace of God in the first place. However, the question remains, often unspoken. It is a fundamental cry of belonging. As they grope for understanding about this heavenly Father who loves them enough to save them from hell, forgive their sins and help them through life, the question remains: "Do You like me as a person?"

Young people know from experience what it means to bear with someone whom you love but who is difficult to like. After all, they are continually figuring out how to cope with their parents' angry, weak and, at times (in their opinion), irrational behavior. No wonder they come to understand God through their own lens of how the world works. It is not only their experience of loving seemingly unenjoyable parents, it is also a personal heart cry. Young people know better than anybody how unenjoyable *they* are, and they can be very raw and honest about expressing that fact. If God knows all, how could He possibly like what He sees?

Confidence is what many lack, yet crave deeply. Some are experts at portraying false confidence, or bravado. They gravitate toward anybody who seems to have overcome insecurity and fear. When they turn their attention to Jesus, they discover that the most powerful, real confidence is found in His presence. The secret that every person on earth is looking for is found within the very power of the Gospel itself, by grace. It is the truth of not just *what* Jesus did for us at the cross, but *why* He did it, and how He feels about us as we begin to believe it and walk in the light of it.

In the midst of immaturity, every young believer on earth longs for confidence. They long to know that Jesus will be gentle with them in their failure. The apostle John wrote very plainly: "We love Him because He first loved us" (1 John 4:19). He gives us, as believers, the power to love Him in the midst of our weakness and brokenness. As young believers encounter His grace, they realize that He is lovable and worth their admiration. This realization grows as they continue to experience His presence, which helps their confidence in the relationship to grow.

I believe that the most prominent and powerful strongholds of our minds are related to the fear of rejection and the trauma of shame. To many Christians, it seems as though they have waited too long to repent or that they have gone too far in sin to be forgiven. Even if they are not being rejected at all, they may feel rejection and shame from God or from those they love, and this apparent fact drains—even devastates—them emotionally.

The hearts of believers will only be satisfied as they grow in the revelation of God's affections. This begins when they come to understand the finished work of the cross. Again, when they understand *what* Jesus did on the cross, then they can begin to comprehend *why* He did it. This seems too good to be true. It is normal to resist this reality until the truth of the Word renews our minds. Then as the presence of God moves our hearts and connects us to truths that are difficult to believe, we grow in our resolve to "go all the way" in loving Jesus.

Jesus very much wants to satisfy our deep longing to be enjoyed. He does this by revealing to us that *He sought us out*. He pursued us. He desired us. Assuredly, He wants a relationship with us. He wants us to comprehend the facts: God came to the earth as the man Jesus purely so that people could respond to His loving pursuit.

The fundamental longing to be loved and enjoyed by God is fulfilled as we receive the revelation about His affection for us. He is the perfect Father and the perfect Bridegroom. He does not love us because He is supposed to. He does not merely tolerate us until we are cleaned up. He draws us closer and closer to Himself the longer we live with Him, and He makes each of us, young and old, able to experience the full measure of His love, so that we can become unshakable in our love for Him. This is what Paul prayed for believers:

> I pray that out of his glorious riches he may strengthen you with power through his Spirit in your inner being, so that Christ may dwell in your hearts through faith. And I pray that you, being rooted and established in love, may have power, together with all the Lord's holy people, to grasp how wide and long and high and deep is the love of Christ, and to know this love that surpasses knowledge—that you may be filled to the measure of all the fullness of God.
>
> Ephesians 3:16–19 NIV

198

Experiencing the Presence of God

To personally and frequently experience the presence of God solves a multitude of problems, big and small. Joy, restoration, healing, power—all come to us through closeness with the One who is intimately near. However, people who do not believe, and therefore who have not experienced the God who both likes and loves them, find it difficult to draw near to Him in worship, prayer and reading the written Word of God. But anyone who believes that God desires a mutual relationship (even though he or she may be immature and "in process" in the spiritual journey) will grow in confidence to pursue God and the richness of His presence.

What does it mean to pursue and experience the "presence of God"? I am saving until the next chapter the idea of pursuing and experiencing the power of God, which is more of an experience of external breakthrough or sudden change when the sovereign hand of God moves powerfully. To pursue the *presence* of God is to pursue an internal breakthrough in one's own heart.

At our new birth in Christ, each of us was given the full measure of His Holy Spirit in our innermost being. We were given a new identity and a glorious new position in relationship with Jesus. And there is nothing like it! However, young believers rarely experience this ongoing reality. They may be filled with the Holy Spirit, but they have yet to experience that fullness as Paul described it: "Now hope does not disappoint, because the love of God has been poured out in our hearts by the Holy Spirit who was given to us" (Romans 5:5).

Enjoying the presence of God is about something so much more than being momentarily moved by God on an emotional level. It is the power of truth connecting deep within our hearts in a way that completely transforms our emotions and desires. The apostle Paul called this "the spirit of wisdom and revelation in the knowledge of Him" (Ephesians 1:17).

Young people want to experience more than the feeling that God loves them. They want to experience the truth of God's affection in a life-changing manner. With their whole future before them, they want His love to make permanent changes in how they view themselves, others, their future and God Himself.

The Christian faith is defined by a number of truly outrageous ideas. We should never become overfamiliar with these ideas. We believe, for example, that the Creator of the universe became a human being who lived among us for a while. We believe that this God-man died by crucifixion, and that He rose from the dead after three days, after which witnesses saw Him ascend to heaven to take His place upon His throne of glory. We believe that, shortly afterward, He sent His Spirit to dwell within His followers. Us. Not only His disciples or the believers who knew Him in the flesh. All of us.

That is an incredible thought. The Holy Spirit of God dwells within us, in fullness. The same God who created everything and who upholds all things and who will restore and renew all things—this God dwells in me. Incalculable power is alive inside of me, the fire of a billion suns. Yet the condition of my heart, my mind and my emotions often makes me forget that He is there. I enjoy union in the deepest part of my being with the Man from Nazareth, but I am content to struggle along without Him.

If I cannot remember that He is ever-present in me, how can I expect to reach out to the next generation with His love? I can share with others only what I am aware that I have in my heart to give.

Pursuing the Presence of God

How can I get better at remembering that He dwells inside me?

My awareness of the presence of the Lord begins, on a daily basis, with simple attentiveness. In other words, the quality of my life in His presence is directly connected to my conscious effort to remember that He is with me. The more I think and talk about Jesus, the more I read or sing Bible passages, the more I will allow His presence to be active in my life. He is right there to help me pursue His presence. Thanks to the Holy Spirit, there is continual activity around my life that I am not fully aware of. God's leadership through the Holy Spirit on my behalf means that day and night He is aiding me. For example, when I do not know how to pray, the Holy Spirit intercedes for me (see Romans 8:26).

As with any relationship, the more I talk to the Lord, the more I will walk with the Lord. Simply remembering that the Spirit of Jesus is alive within me is an act of faith that positions me to experience more of His leadership and power in my life. The more I connect to His Spirit, the more I will engage with Jesus.

He wants us to ask Him for things. As Jesus Himself told us, "Ask, and it will be given to you; seek, and you will find; knock, and it will be opened to you" (Matthew 7:7). When I start to think that I am asking too much or that He will not want to bother with me, I need to review James' admonition: "You do not have because you do not ask" (James 4:2 NASB). This is one of the simplest of scriptural principles: the more you ask for, the more you will experience walking with God, within His will.

In my own experience (and in Jesus' words, recorded in the Bible), I must become like a child.[1] Without the childlike attitude of humility, simplicity and dependency, I will conduct my life busily, without even thinking about God. I will become so task-oriented and me-oriented that I will forget that Jesus died in order for each of us to become we-oriented.

He offers me infinite capacity to grow and mature in my relationship with Him. With the eternal God fighting on my behalf—and actually dwelling within me—I have more than enough help to overcome all obstacles to godliness. If I am to love Jesus back with a tender, responsive heart of thanksgiving, I have to do so on His terms. His terms are the ones that propel my new life, and they work much better than my terms. Therefore, I have to contend for the three heart attitudes listed above—humility, simplicity and dependency—because when all three are working in tandem, they will subdue my independent thinking, my prideful love of my own opinions and my own distorted sense of self-righteousness. I can see Jesus—and myself—more clearly and with more objectivity. I can approach Him without shame and with confidence that I am loved. In the process, I receive real power from His Spirit to grow in love.

The Rewards of His Presence

The more I connect with the presence of the Lord through prayer, the more active His leadership will be in my life. I will notice simple things. Sermons will start to make sense in ways they never did before. Phrases people say—little snippets of counsel and godly wisdom—will stick in my mind and heart and refuse to let go. I will notice that Jesus' ideas are transforming my perspective and altering my emotions for the better. I will begin to believe things that I used to deny. I will see things—about myself, about others, even about my enemies—that I could not see before. I will have far more patience for the weakness and brokenness of others than I used to have earlier in my journey with Christ. A thousand incremental changes will steadily take hold of my heart. Without being able to pinpoint the exact moment when it all changed, I will find that I am radically different. It is well worth the effort to pursue the presence of God!

After a while, something else happens that is quite glorious: His presence, values and affections will begin to permeate my ministry. That will make my ministry much more effective, because the only things I can say or do that will ever reach the hearts of others are the things that have touched my heart as a minister. I will want more than anything to share with others about this God who loves us all so thoroughly and who can do so much.

Thus transformed, I will become zealous for others to be transformed in the same manner. I want those around me to "taste and see" the same goodness from God that has so awakened my heart (Psalm 34:8).

As the presence of God transforms my life, then transforms my ministry philosophy and then transforms those I minister to, I had better realize that the next generation of believers does not need *me*. They need Jesus. They need something far beyond what I could ever give. My gifts, my personal charisma and my organizational abilities cannot answer the deepest needs of the human heart. I must simply introduce them to Jesus and help them to stay with Him. I can share my journey with them and tell them my stories. I can give them practical ways to serve others. I can help them understand the Bible. Through it all, they must seek for and experience His presence for themselves, or nothing significant will happen in their lives.

It is imperative that I continue to prioritize the presence of God in my own life and ministry, expecting to see the power of God touch the hearts of the next generation more than I aim for effective programs and growth.

How to Prioritize the Presence of God

Once the presence of God in our lives and ministries becomes a priority in our hearts, how do we follow through on this desire? I can think of three practical and powerful ways: We must sing the Scriptures, we must disciple people to be fascinated with Jesus and we must train the next generation to connect with Jesus.

Sing the Scriptures

Saint Augustine (AD 430) is credited with the saying, "*Qui bene cantat bis orat*." This means, "He who sings well prays twice."[2] More to my point, he also said, "Singing belongs to the one who loves." The Spirit of God rides best on the chariot of the Word of God, and singing the Word of God is the best way of all to express the love song of our hearts—and transform our deepest emotions in the process.

Why music? The mystery of music is in the being of God Himself. Why? God is a musician, and in Revelation chapter 4, we get a glimpse of how music surrounds and fills the place of His heavenly throne. Around the throne of God, the saints and angels rejoice in the Holy Spirit with music and singing as they worship before the Father. A musical God created the human spirit to be musical as well.

Music is the key to positioning our hearts to experience the presence of God. Thus, it is vital to discipleship, to our ministries and to all of the work we do. In 1703 a Scottish politician named Andrew Fletcher asserted that "if a man were permitted to make all the ballads, he need not care who should make the laws of a nation."[3] In other words, songs are much more than entertainment; they also inform good decision-making.

Christians may not be able to break down the theological details about propitiation or justification, but singing escorts their hearts into an encounter with truth that is greater than their understanding. A whole room filled with diverse believers who disagree on many things can still feel the same things together through music. Even one hundred thousand people in a stadium can enter into the same depth of emotion together, experiencing the same truths together for hours at a time with the combination of anointed musical worship and anointed preaching. The worshipers can feel God's truth so deeply that it helps them understand it. In addition, the songs soften their hearts to enter ever more deeply into God's presence.

Disciples Fascinated with Jesus

Secondly, we must disciple people to be fascinated with Jesus. Our teaching and preaching content must expand to reflect who Jesus is, what He is like and the details of how He loves us. As we introduce new believers to experiencing His presence, we can help them move from being attracted to Him to loving Him to being captivated by Him.

Every human spirit carries a capacity for marvel. Because of our divine design, we require a sense of wonderment in the core of our beings. Unless we have a sense of awe, we live aimlessly and spiritually bored, and a spiritually bored Church is weak and vulnerable to Satan. A fascinated believer, on the other hand, is strong and equipped to face temptation. King David was passionate about God even as he was occupied with leading the nation of Israel. He expressed his heart in a song: "One thing I have desired . . . all the days of my life, to behold the beauty of the LORD" (Psalm 27:4).

The secular entertainment industry has identified this human longing and has targeted it commercially. They have exploited it to their own profit—and to our ruin. People search in vain through secular entertainment and recreation to fulfill their God-given craving for fascination.

There is a growing cry from the next generation to fully commit themselves to pursuing, knowing and encountering Jesus. The declaration of King David for his life to be about "one thing" only is shared by young men and women across the Body of Christ today. They want to become preoccupied with God while their hands are occupied with their ministry for Him. God offers His grace to anyone who wants to know His glory.

Knowing truths about Jesus awakens us to reach out to know Him more. It is so much more than knowing *about* Jesus; it is knowing the Man Jesus deeply and fully. We were all made for this pursuit. The presence of the Lord becomes meaningful and precious to us when objective truth informs our thoughts and emotions. This is especially essential for young believers. The more new believers knows about Jesus, the more they will be able to stand confidently before Jesus. As they do, they begin to value and desire times of worship more than the social and recreational entertainment.

I have seen this firsthand. I have been involved with youth ministries where the knowledge of God and music and corporate singing were valued highly. Time and time again, I have watched as bored, distracted and disconnected young people come to life, awakened by God's grace to the beauty of who Jesus is. I have watched them give Him their all with tears of delight, singing and presenting their hearts to God. There are few things on earth that are more beautiful to me than the sight of a young person opening his or her heart to God, confident in and exhilarated by His love.

I think we tend to draw back from introducing young people to the presence of God because we fear failure. It is hard for us to imagine that teenagers and young adults will be up for the challenge. However, for twenty years I have found the opposite to be true. The next generation of young people is hungry for both the knowledge of God and the presence of God. They want to be fascinated by Him for the rest of their lives.

A Praying Generation

Finally, we must train the next generation to connect with Jesus. This is the most difficult but most rewarding part.

This is a potentially intimidating task for busy teachers, fathers and mothers, because it means not only calling others to prayer, but actually developing a strong personal prayer life. However, that is only the beginning of the challenge. Keeping others before the Lord in prayer over decades is the task of a lifetime, especially if a leader is attempting to get those others to pray consistently as well. Yet here we are discussing biblical preparation for the hour in which we find ourselves. The centerpiece of our discussion must be our own prayer lives and the prayer lives of those we are discipling.

Therefore, as our revelation about the urgency of the hour increases, our desire for prayer must increase as well. A godly believer who desires something eternal for those under his or her care must do more than lift up a few hasty prayers on the run between meetings and events. It takes something beyond praying sporadically from a sense of duty more than true devotion.

A PRAYER-FRIENDLY CULTURE

What captures the imagination of Christians who long for the people around them to encounter God is something more holistic in nature: a culture of prayer. More than a prayer life or a prayer meeting, a prayer culture speaks of a praying people. The act of prayer in a praying culture is structured and scheduled as well as spontaneous and organic. The believers who are blessed to be a part of a culture of prayer are those who run after more of God in their lives in an environment conducive to pursuit.

It is surprising how regularly church culture can accidentally work against a wholehearted pursuit of Jesus. A prayer culture, however, facilitates and encourages it.

When you are building a culture that encourages, sustains and equips other people in prayer, that success flows directly from your prayer life. The values that you possess—*why* you pray related to *what* you value—are far more important in building a prayer culture than *how* you pray.

In teaching His Church how to pray, Jesus gave us a model of prayer based on what God is like and on the nature of the Kingdom (see Matthew 6:9–13). Jesus' prayer model covered all the foundational basics that are expanded on throughout Scripture. He told us the things that we must know and keep central in our quest to grow strong in prayer.

Jesus' teaching on prayer starts with a strong focus on who God is; He is our Father in heaven and developing a right view of God as our heavenly Father is foundational to a strong prayer life. A. W. Tozer insisted that a low view of God has been the biggest problem in the Church in every generation:

It is my opinion that the Christian conception of God current in these middle years of the twentieth century is so decadent as to be utterly beneath the dignity of the Most High God and actually to constitute for professed believers something amounting to a moral calamity. All the problems of heaven and earth, though they were to confront us together and at once, would be nothing compared with the overwhelming problem of God: That He is; what He is like; and what we as moral beings must do about Him.[4]

As we pray, we must intentionally take time to recall who He is according to His Word. Therefore, teaching on who God is and how He feels about us becomes central to building a culture that is conducive to prayer. Our worship and love for Jesus will never surpass our knowledge of Him. We will misunderstand the call to worship if we fail to understand Jesus' majesty. Where the vision of Jesus is lacking, deep and continual worship and prayer will be lacking. Jesus Himself asked, "Who do you say that I am?" (Matthew 16:15). When we know Jesus for who He is, it makes sense to adore Him continually, regardless of the cost.

The Lord is worthy of unceasing worship in heaven and on earth. He desires to be worshiped on earth as He is in heaven. Worship is primary because Jesus is preeminent, and worship is both an end and a means to an end. Jesus' infinite beauty is enough to warrant our extravagant and continual worship. After all, the angelic host worships because they see His greatness, not because they have been forgiven for sin, healed physically or provided for financially. Worship, in other words, is a response to the revelation of God. All who encounter His beauty respond in worship.

Thus, sustaining the effort it takes to grow deep in the knowledge of God is the key to sustaining a culture of prayer, because a culture of prayer is built upon the foundation of knowing God and being loved by Him.

In a culture of prayer, God must be desirable and prayer must be doable. The two goals of a leader involve cultivating confidence in the love of God and constant conversation with the Lord. Simple, short phrases from prayers from the Bible itself makes prayer much simpler, and adding the dimension of music makes prayer more enjoyable and sustainable. This works with individuals at home in their bedrooms, and it also helps facilitate prayer meetings. In fact, when people pray consistently in their bedrooms it becomes easier for them to pray well together. And a culture of prayer must include regular times of corporate prayer.

A PRAYING PEOPLE

Worship and intercession are set forth as supremely important to God's Kingdom throughout all of history. In fact, human history began with daily prayer meetings in the Garden of Eden (see Genesis 3:8). The nation of Israel began in a prayer meeting at Mt. Sinai (see Exodus 19:6–20). Israel's first building project was to build a worship sanctuary (see Exodus 25:8). God set apart an entire tribe (the Levites) in Israel to maintain day-and-night worship. David established night-and-day worship in Jerusalem providing full-time financing for over four thousand musicians and singers in the tabernacle of David (see 1 Chronicles 23:5). The early Church began and operated in prayer meetings (see Acts 2:42). And natural history will end in the context of a powerful global prayer movement.

Many passages of Scripture provide for us a clear picture of diverse cultures, peoples groups and nations reconciled in Christ, enjoying and engaging with Yahweh together through the vehicle of prayer and worship.[5] Unceasing adoration of

Christ via worship and prayer is the optimum context to bring a diverse people together into enjoyable engagement with Jesus under the government of God. That is why building a culture of prayer among believers is the primary way to bring God's people into full maturity in love.[6] The goals of a praying people are three:

To labor in intercession: Night-and-day prayer are required for the full release of justice in the Church and society. Worship and prayer change the spiritual atmosphere of the region being prayed for, and continual prayer releases the Spirit to move in a greater measure. Thus, the works of the Kingdom can have a greater impact. Jesus spoke about this: "Will not God bring about justice for His elect *who cry to Him day and night* . . . ? He will bring about justice for them. . . . When the Son of Man comes, *will He find faith on the earth?*" (Luke 18:7–8 NASB, emphasis added).

To encounter God: Prayer positions us to receive more from the Holy Spirit—to experience more of God's grace to know, love and obey Jesus in a deeper way. In worship, we align our heart with Him and we receive more from Him. Jesus has so much to say to us. He wants a two-way relationship. It is the nature of God to communicate His heart with His people.

To grow in revelation of the Word: Through the Scripture, we see the majesty of God as our Father and the majesty of Jesus as Bridegroom, King and Judge. We gain insight into His will, ways and plans. We come to understand the unique dynamics of His end-time plan to transition the earth to the age to come.

Believers can be trained to grow in these three areas as they develop a life in prayer with other believers. First, we must lay hold of a vision to move those we are equipping and discipling beyond occasional prayer, helping them instead to become a praying people for whom prayer becomes their default. Through a life of prayer, we overcome pressure, relate tenderly to God and find grace to love others well on a daily basis. This is, in my opinion, the most critical component of preparing our hearts and our lives for the coming storm of glory and the rage of the nations.

11

Burning and Shining Lamps

I hope reading this book has encouraged you to grow in your desire to help Christians be prepared for the future, enabling them to endure in long-suffering love. Our fruitfulness in service also involves laboring to provide a spiritual inheritance. A broken world is aching for true fathers and mothers in the faith who carry with them the fragrance of Christ. These are the people who have paid a great hidden price, overcoming offenses, resisting bitterness and disappointment, persevering in the face of temptation and deprivation. The greatest need in the Body of Christ in this darkening hour is for people who will walk in this manner, who are not concerned so much about being heard or taken seriously as much as they are in shining from the inside with the love of Jesus.

These people have chosen the way of the heart. They have embraced quietness, contemplation and a life of prayer. They have fought for "oil on the inside," and as they have aged, they have grown in tenderness of heart rather than in bitterness and disappointment. They are fighting the good fight with a "good eye," as Jesus taught in the Sermon on the Mount, living before an audience of One rather than seeking the attention and approval of other people, even others in the Body of Christ.

These are the fathers and mothers who have gone the way of ancient saints, who truly encountered God in prayer. Continually, they pursue new awakenings of the glory, abandoned to Him for life, always mining the potential of prayer, communion and friendship with God. They always look for the deep reality of love in Christ, pushing aside mere rhetoric and sentimentality.

These men and women belong to the company of John the Baptist, who was known as the "friend of the bridegroom" (see John 3:20–30). They are the nameless and faceless people who are unconcerned about personal gain or platform or huge influence. Their hearts are fascinated with Jesus' beauty, and they want nothing more than to keep preparing their hearts so that they can partner with Jesus to prepare the way for His return. They are steadfast in this desire, and they are unoffendable because they have laid down their lives.

These are the "burning and shining" people who carry within them a brightness of life and joy that can only come by entering into deep and intimate friendship with Jesus.

Seeking the Fullness of God Together

The Father is jealous to have us to Himself, to make each of us everything that we can be by His grace. He sees the fullness of who we were made to be. He sees the potential for love and holiness deep within our hearts; He put the seeds of that potential there according to His divine design. His heart burns with an intense fire of desire to see us come into His fullness. He is committed to bringing each of us into our glorious potential. When we draw back from Him through lethargy or compromise, He does not draw back from us. He does not get frustrated like earthly fathers. Holy, jealous love fuels Him, and He is always looking to bring about our good. He remains joyful and confident as well as kind and compassionate, refusing to settle for less than our fullness.

The Lord disciplines us in order to fulfill His great promises (see Hebrews 12:3–11). We can be discouraged by the Lord's chastisements because we misinterpret it as His disappointment or disapproval. Viewing chastisement through an earthly lens, we imagine that a frustrated Father is correcting and disciplining us with impatience toward our sin and weakness.

But our loving Father seeks to break off whatever hinders us from our future promises. He chastens us for our profit, that we might ultimately be partakers in His holiness, which includes walking in deeper unity and partnership with Jesus, and the chastisement comes in answer to our prayers for a deeper relationship with Jesus.

Here is how it works: I pray and ask God to lead me into the fullness of His promises, and God takes my prayers very seriously. He responds to my request by stepping in to set things right. He cannot allow me to enter into His promises until I have been prepared by His chastening and correction. Without it, I will be completely unprepared for the intensity of the difficulties that come with His glory.

I cannot emphasize this enough. His grace is sufficient, and He is fully committed to bringing all of us the whole way, in love: "He who began a good work in you will carry it on to completion until the day of Christ Jesus" (Philippians 1:6 NIV).

The Father's desire is to build a spiritual family or culture on the earth that values Jesus for His own sake and that speaks often of the fullness of God with overflowing gratitude. By "fullness of God," I mean a life of deep communion with the Spirit. This is a "fasted life," a life of self-sacrifice, for the sake of cultivating the most important relationship in the universe, our divine romance with God Himself. To be filled and refilled with His presence, I need to limit myself in my daily activities so that I can slow down enough to devote time to seeking Him out and experiencing His touch. What a paradigm shift this represents for almost everyone in the Western world today. We must learn how to value the interior life with Jesus. At the same time, this is not a solitary pursuit. He called you so that you could find a place within His Body and thrive there. We lay hold of this new world *together*.

This is the full potential of the Bride. I am eager for us to go forward in Him, together.

There is more; there is always more, and I am hungry to lay hold of what is possible by the grace of God. Together, how can we follow the Father better? How can we become a global family, united in our calling and our identity and what we are about as a people? Together, we can reach our destination. Separately, we will flounder. We are like a ship trying to find true north again, and we can set sail with confidence even if some of the crew members are still in training. We are on this journey together.

Friendship with a Bridegroom God

We need the Word of God to come to us, to invade our hearts and lives (see Luke 3:2). We cannot simply resolve to "do better" or "try harder" in our Christianity. This is not about being better parents, friends or individuals. We need God to conquer our hearts with love and to unlock our full potential as a praying and fasting people. Together, we must share with those new to our family exciting stories of friendship with God through prayer and encountering Jesus in His Word.

The way forward is the way of John the Baptist. "He who has the bride is the bridegroom; but the friend of the bridegroom, who stands and hears him, rejoices greatly because of the bridegroom's voice. Therefore this joy of mine is fulfilled" (John 3:29).

This is the central reality of the Kingdom. We want to be people who stand before the Lord with our Bibles open, who lean in to hear His voice. Those who seek to serve and love well in the days ahead must take hold of this reality in a fresh way and keep doing it as we move forward. How greatly we need the power of God to move into our lives to give us strength to persevere! We need His grace to overcome frustrations and difficulties today, and persecution and crisis tomorrow. God's answer to the coming crisis that will engulf the whole world is a sizable company of dear friends who can move in great power, secured by deep intimacy, fueled by their love for Him. As we labor, we need to be both urgently alert and quietly refreshed by our daily encounter with the living God.

John wrote, "He who *has* the bride is the bridegroom," because he understood the great eternal plan of God, which was to provide His Son with an eternal companion, a Bride with whom He could be equally yoked. We do not often think of this as one of the most powerful and glorious themes of all of Scripture, but it is. And it is one of the most powerful statements that can be made about our value and dignity when we are well-joined to Christ. Let's remind each other often that you

217

and I are important to Jesus the Bridegroom because together we are being established as His Bride.

As the Bridegroom, Jesus has tender love and burns with jealous desire for His people. As the Bride of the Bridegroom King, we are expected to share in the deep things of His heart (His emotions and His thoughts). There is no relationship of greater intimacy and intensity than that of a husband and wife. Thus, to enjoy active intimacy with Jesus includes sharing the desires of His heart, His affection and His thoughts. Our knowledge of our unity with Him gives us great courage as we walk into the future (see 1 Corinthians 2:10–12). His affection beautifies our hearts in love and humility.

The Holy Spirit beckons us to enjoy intimacy with God by enabling us to experience the deep things of God. The Spirit discerns the deep things of God's heart (emotions), His mind (plans) and His power (works of creation, redemption, the new Jerusalem and more) so that we might know and experience them. God opens His heart to make it possible for us to experience active intimacy with Him. This is our inheritance and destiny in Christ, and it goes far beyond superficial Christian religion. Experiencing intimacy with God's heart energizes our hearts with His beauty, love and power, outstripping the dullness and distraction of our daily task lists (see Ephesians 3:16–19).

Partnership as a betrothed Bride means that we live in the context of a soon-coming wedding—or what King Solomon called the "day of the gladness of his heart" (Song of Solomon 3:11). Although we must prepare to endure much hardship in the future time, we are preparing for something far more glorious; Christian believers are making themselves ready for the day that is most dear to the heart of Jesus. The day of His gladness contextualizes our labors and sets them in the midst of the urgency of wedding preparations and the storm of His jealousy to return for His beloved ones.

Understanding the hours in which we live means we know what this is "unto" and what it is all for. With thankful and tender hearts, let's work toward the day of the fullness of His gladness and overflowing joy.

John the Baptist described himself as being "the friend of the bridegroom, who stands and hears him." He likened himself to the best man in a wedding, who does not seek to attract the bride's attention and affections but who works to prepare her to receive the embrace of the bridegroom.

Paul spoke of people who showcase themselves. Friends of the Bridegroom do not operate that way; instead, they prepare people to receive Jesus' embrace as the Bridegroom, empowering them to walk out the first commandment: "You shall love the LORD your God with all your heart, with all your soul, and with all your mind" (Matthew 22:37). Like John, they see their identity as being wrapped up in friendship with Jesus as the *Bridegroom*. They carry close to their hearts the greatest desires of Jesus. They will contend for what He longs for, even if it means personal hardship. They will not make claims on the loyalty of others, but will always point to the Bridegroom. They will not cause people to look to them for security, provision or protection, but will simply point them to the beauty and the majesty of Jesus.

As a friend of the Bridegroom "who stands," we will stand in God's presence in prayer and with diligent attention to His Word. This kind of standing indicates that we will lean into Him in any setting in which the Lord wants to speak and reveal Himself, such as teaching sessions, Bible studies, conversations or prayer meetings. We need to ask ourselves: Are we awake, attentive, reaching and leaning forward with a grace-awakened hunger and longing for Him? Are we leaning in with expectation of seeing more of His life as we glimpse His beauty in His Word? "For who has stood in the counsel of the LORD, and has perceived and heard His word? Who has marked His word and heard it?" (Jeremiah 23:18).

As a friend of the Bridegroom "who hears him," we respond, individually and corporately, with wholehearted obedience regardless of the price. We are living in a season of preparation, kind of a "reset" season in which the Lord is speaking in intimate and powerful ways. We hear the Lord by working to apply what He is saying to our own lives with sincere humility and repentance.

The friend of the Bridegroom "rejoices greatly because of the bridegroom's voice," and he says, "Therefore this joy of mine is fulfilled." Even in the midst of the difficulties of a rigorous lifestyle, John was empowered with joy by receiving the revelation of the Bridegroom. Whether we are going through seasons of increase or decrease, our joy is rooted in something "other." This joy fastens our affections on Jesus and sustains us in every season regardless of difficulty or pressure. Let's keep embracing this joy today, as the very real pressure grows, and even more in the days to come.

John the Baptist spent seventeen years alone in the wilderness, praying and fasting. What did that accomplish? John declares boldly, "I have heard the voice of the Bridegroom." When we, too, hear His voice, we will not mistake who He is, and we will not hesitate to follow Him wherever He is going. His voice tells us that He takes pleasure and delight in us, and that settles all of our identity issues.

It is written about Jesus in Hebrews 12:2 that for the joy set before Him, He endured the cross. What is "the joy"? It is the joy of a Bridegroom rejoicing over a Bride. That same joy empowered John the Baptist. The joy of the bridal revelation helped John endure the privations of the wilderness so that he could emerge with a world-changing message.

This same joy will help us endure the present and coming difficulties. We can hear the voice of God through the Word of God, which touches our hearts and redefines our thinking. His voice gives us our own spiritual identity, and it shows us how we should perceive Him. We must see ourselves as a cherished Bride on the way to ascend a throne, indescribably beautiful to the Son of God, and cherished. Missed opportunities, mistreatment or misunderstanding cannot rob us of our true joy. This is who we are.

"He must increase, but I must decrease," said John the Baptist (John 3:30). God does not reward anything that He does not establish. Those things do not stand up under trials or pressures anyway. So much of the anxiety in life today is in vain, as too many of God's people try to receive something that heaven has not promised them. Let's decrease. Let's forget about gaining influence through human striving and self-driven networking to build a name and a platform, because none of that will last at the throne of God.

John was not anxious about his ministry decreasing. Many of his disciples started to follow Jesus. As Jesus began to go about teaching and working miracles, the attention was going to Him. John knew that he should not prop up something that heaven was not promoting anymore. His time of active ministry was ending, and he needed to decrease so that Jesus' name could be exalted. As friends of the Bridegroom, we must imitate John.

How much energy have you and I wasted chasing something that God has not given or trying to prop up something that God has not established? Let's encourage each other to keep our eyes on Jesus exclusively, and to abandon our own efforts in favor of doing whatever He is doing.

Years of fasting and prayer have only awakened me all the more to the war on the inside of myself—I know that whole-hearted love is right and that Jesus is worthy of it, yet on the inside a very real part of me does not want to give up anything further or reach for anything more. I am at war within myself. Jesus knows this, and He knows how to win: by conquering my heart with His love.

The Body of Christ has an odd and glorious assignment to fulfill together: to be a corporate John the Baptist. By the grace of God, an entire generation will step together into the culmination of the story. This is high and beyond us, way out of our reach, almost unimaginable. But the Bridegroom is fully committed to bringing us together into our destiny in and with Him. He makes the impossible possible!

Moving forward together, remembering what He has done in the past, we grow in faith regarding what He will do at the climax of history. We allow Him to lay hold of us, so that we as His Bride can lay hold of Him together. In doing so, we establish a glorious witness of His beauty for all the nations to see, that they might believe and repent before the great and terrible day of the Lord (see Joel 2:11).

12

Counted Worthy
of This Calling

Paul's prayer for the saints in Thessalonica is one of the most surprising and incredible prayers in the New Testament:

> Therefore we also pray always for you that our God would count you worthy of this calling, and fulfill all the good pleasure of His goodness and the work of faith with power, that the name of our Lord Jesus Christ may be glorified in you, and you in Him, according to the grace of our God and the Lord Jesus Christ.
>
> 2 Thessalonians 1:11–12

The context of this prayer is the persecution of the Thessalonian church at the hands of wicked men. Remarkably, Paul is not praying for them to be delivered or spared from their suffering. He is not praying that it will stop. To the contrary, Paul is presenting the idea that the godly, humble faith of the saints, who are under great pressure, will be vindicated when they see the beauty of Jesus.

In other words, Paul understands that their suffering will not be in vain and, in fact, will be worth it all when they see Him in His revealed glory and power. Moreover, He will be glorified in the saints who stood firm in their love and devotion to Him even in the face of oppression, suffering and injustice. Paul prays that they would be able to fulfill this calling on their lives: the call to display for all to see, by their steadfastness and sacrificial love, the matchless and incomparable worth of Christ.

Paul's prayer is a prayer for them to come into the fullness of what they were made for as believers: to experience and express the deep, jealous, fiery and sacrificial love of Jesus. Paul is praying a prayer of full abandonment to the cause of wholehearted love—a prayer for maturity and deep personal assent to God's good plans and purposes.

The Thessalonian believers were persecuted, suffering lovers of Jesus Christ. Such hardship always raises the question of whether or not the suffering will be worth it. Paul is praying that they will be able to walk in the fullness of their calling with deep conviction and power to overcome all doubt, despair and fear. He is praying that their steadfast love might display to the world the way of a better Kingdom and better King.

If Paul were to pray a similar prayer for us, he would pray that we would be able to walk in the fullness of our calling by doing what He joyfully sent us here to do according to His sovereign purposes, and that we would walk forward with deep conviction and fresh power, persevering in what we do together.

In our pursuit of spiritual maturity, we are strengthened in love by our daily declaration that it is and will be worth all the effort. His promises are worth giving our lives for. If we slip into doubting the worth of our personal sacrifices and obedience, we may falter, because even raising the question "Is this worth it?" will wreak havoc in our hearts. Is all the hassle and hardship worth it? Is it worth it to endure the pain, the rejection and all of the endless waiting?

I believe that on the other side of all of the hardships is a spectacular day of vindication and justification. In that day, the name of the Lord Jesus Christ will be glorified in the faithful intercessor, and the faithful intercessor will be glorified in Him. After the revival appears, the finances move, the power comes and the bodies are healed, everyone will remember and honor the simple, humble people who believed God, who prayed and fasted until He came. If there are reproaches or accusations against the many, many faithful saints from around the world who are and have been (and many more that will be) a key part of God's future breakthrough into His promises, He will silence them all in the days to come, as He vindicates His own name.

The only way to be found worthy of your calling is to be prepared by grace to both endure and step into God's promises without losing your way. You will need oil for your lamp (tenderness and responsiveness to God), the anchor of simplicity and humility, and the dream of loving God with your whole heart in genuine abandonment. This is what glorifies Jesus and puts Him on display for the nations to behold—the saints of God stepping forward steadily and humbly into the storm of controversy.

In faith, we want to ask for a divine escort of the Holy Spirit into a place of abandonment; we want to get lost in His great love that we have not yet touched. This invitation and wonderful inheritance belong to every member of the spiritual family of God who hears and believes. Let's throw ourselves at His feet and surrender our hearts to Him!

The Western Church and Malachi 4:5–6

I believe that the Church in the Western world is at a critical point. As I look around the Body of Christ, I see two troubling trends. First, I see pastors and leaders advancing in age, having faithfully served their people, their congregations and their movements for many decades. Yet either they have no spiritual sons or daughters to whom to pass the baton, or they are financially incapable of doing so. Therefore, their congregations, ministries and movements are aging along with them, a few decades away from quietly fading from memory. Sixty- and seventy-year-old fathers are sharing their wisdom and seasoned perspective with fifty- and sixty-year-old audiences. The younger men and women who desperately need their measured and sober perspective are elsewhere, finding their own way in the world.

Then there is a second point of concern: In both denominational and nondenominational settings, it is becoming more and more common to see churches, as their leaders retire, handing their ministries over to very young, very inexperienced leaders. The aim is to secure the future by setting younger leadership into place, which leads to having younger congregants, young families, vibrant children's ministries and more. (It is understood that, as a rule, leaders can effectively lead people a decade younger and a decade older; very few can lead a broader cross section of people.)

Elsewhere, young leaders are finding their own ways to circumvent the old systems and the outdated demands they place on releasing young leaders into ministry and church leadership. Newer church-planting methodologies and marketing systems allow for young leaders to be propelled into successful church planting without deferring to the older boards, outdated models and the resistance of older congregants.

Churches are being planted! Churches are growing! Young leaders are finding success! Perhaps the things that are dying should die, so what is the problem here?

In Malachi 4:5, the prophet Malachi promised that the Lord would send "Elijah the prophet before the coming of the great and dreadful day of the LORD." The Lord will do so, according to Malachi, in order to "turn the hearts of the fathers to the children, and the hearts of the children to their fathers, lest I come and strike the earth with a curse" (verse 6).

The Church of the Western world now finds itself in this critical moment. This key moment of history involves fathers and sons, mothers and daughters, and the connection of three generations of faith. We are on the brink of historic economic, social, moral and societal changes that have staggering implications for the world as we understand it. We find ourselves with an almost desperate need for spiritual men and women of depth, seasoning, battle-tested perspective and experience, people who can point the Church to the things that really matter in a world of shallow options and misplaced cultural optimism. The world urgently needs a Church with wisdom and revelation that can express the authentic heart and mind of Christ.

Young adults in their twenties represent the vibrancy, health and future of the Church. These young believers, stewarding their new families into the faith with passion, are a beautiful and central expression of the life of the Church as it engages the world around it. Thirty- and forty-year-old pastors and leaders are surely the strength of ministry organizations, able to lead, pastor and organize the advance of the Kingdom, using their gifts and abilities to connect people to values that keep them loving Jesus when pain, discouragement and difficulty make staying with the faith exceedingly difficult. Sixty- and seventy-year-old fathers and mothers in the faith, however—the men and women with history and depth, tested and tried yet faithful and unoffended—this group should not be neglected. Their contributions are profoundly necessary to the maintenance of the vibrant health of spiritual communities. They serve as the wise tiebreakers in the arguments of younger leaders, who have differing opinions regarding success and the things that matter.

In our world today, the generational gap has widened, and the cultural rift between young and old has found its way into the Church. The old processes of advancement and promotion in the professional world have changed. Twenty- and thirty-year-olds no longer want or need the positions, permissions, experience or resources of an older generation to acquire wealth and achieve success in the modern world. Advanced degrees mean less; experience means more. And the kind of experience that counts in today's economy, in the midst of breathtaking technological advancements, belongs to the younger generation.

As the younger generation and the older generation engage with each other less and less in the professional world, mentorship, training and even a seasoned perspective are being passed down less frequently. This is now becoming true within the Church as well; older systems of professional entry and advancement into the denominational roles are rapidly becoming dated and irrelevant. No longer are as many young leaders undergoing approval testing by their denominations to determine if they are fit to serve within churches and ministries. Seminary education may or may not be required. Many younger leaders who enter into the ministry come to their roles in nontraditional ways that are outside of the old norms.

The great downside to this new expression of the generation gap is when one generation declares to another, "I have no need of you." Sixty- and seventy-year-old fathers and mothers have clarity and sober-minded perspective but forty-year-old leaders have the seasoned strength and resources, while at the same time twenty-year-old leaders have the time and the energy to run hard with passion. Who should be in charge? Which way should you run? How far is the journey?

The answers to these questions and the will to execute the answers can be found only in a cross-generational expression of *family*, undergirded by humility and deep gratitude to the Lord for His mercy and grace.

How do we engage three generations at once, preparing together for the victory of God in the days ahead? We build a culture of prayer together. We build this in our homes, with our families. We reach for Jesus in the gaps of our day, in the empty spaces as we move from here to there. We reach together. We listen together. We talk about God together. We keep our hearts alive as we watch the Good Shepherd build the family of God worldwide.

It is important to reemphasize that God desires a *praying family* that engages together with His heart. The kind of spiritual family that we must build together, as expressed earlier, involves a culture of prayer. Again, and most crucially, a culture of prayer is built upon the foundation of knowing God and being loved by Him.

To review, in teaching His Church how to pray, Jesus gave us a model of prayer based on what God is like and on the nature of the Kingdom (see Matthew 6:9–13). Jesus' prayer model covered all the foundational basics that are expanded upon throughout Scripture. He told us the things that we must keep central in our quest to grow strong in prayer.

As we pray, we must intentionally take time to recall who He is according to His Word. This enables us to build a culture that is conducive to prayer. Our worship and love for Jesus will never surpass our knowledge of Him. The revelation of God and its result—the subsequent inevitable fascination with Him—are the very foundation of the worship movement. Thus, sustaining the effort it takes to grow deep in the knowledge of God is the key to sustaining a culture of prayer.

When we know Jesus as He truly is, it makes sense to adore Him continually, regardless of the cost.

The Lord is worthy of unceasing worship in heaven and on earth. He desires to be worshiped on earth as He is in heaven. Worship is primary because Jesus is preeminent. Worship is both an end and a means to an end. Worship is the ultimate goal of the Church and of all its missions. Jesus' infinite beauty is enough to warrant the extravagant and continual worship of His Church. After all, this is why the angelic host worships; they do not worship Him for the limited reasons of many of us, such as being forgiven for sin, healed physically or provided for financially. They see only one thing: His greatness.

And all who encounter His beauty will respond in worship—we can be sure of that.

In Closing

Throughout this book, I have been operating on a number of premises that I believe to be true. First, I have a strong conviction that we are living in one of the most unique generations in all of history. Spiritually, biblically, sociologically, politically, economically and beyond, there has never been a generation like this one. This is true, as we have seen, in the positive dimensions of prayer, missions and the work of the Holy Spirit worldwide. This is also true, as I have tried to present, in the negative dimension of anti-Christian thought and expression worldwide that seeks the conformity or removal of Christianity as we know it today. We have arrived, in my observation, at a uniquely glorious and perilous hour of history.

I also believe that the greatest days for the Body of Christ are yet ahead of us. I have a strong conviction that the greatest revival in human history is coming, and that billions of souls will be swept powerfully into the Kingdom of God by the unprecedented display of the power of the Holy Spirit.

This is not a unique view. There are many that have been proclaiming similar things recently, and this encourages me greatly.

What is unique, in my observation, is my next premise: that global revival is going to cause an explosion of global shaking in the nations and tribulation for the Church unlike anything any of us have ever seen, the scope of which is almost impossible to believe. Yet this premise is based on what the Bible lays out. Scripture is clear in declaring that the rage of the nations and the judgments of the Lord are ahead for us all.

Therefore, it is my conviction that extreme times call for extreme measures. We cannot continue to live as if tomorrow will be like today. We cannot pretend that the world around us is not growing darker and angrier. I can see that the anger is seething within the Church, not only outside of it. We cannot maintain business as usual and be content to merely put a sunny face on a happy message. This just will not do.

I find it irresponsible to prophesy, "Revival!" and do nothing to prepare the next generation for it. I find it irresponsible to proclaim hope and positivity and do little to alert the saints to the severity of the times and failing to equip them for their necessary response. The time is at hand for fervent responses that arise from persistent prayer. The days that I have long seen approach our shores have now arrived. The future is now, and dark and troubling days are upon us.

Even now, as economic uncertainty and difficulty has begun to unfold in the world around us while we wrestle with an unprecedented world crisis, well-meaning voices of positivity seek to deliver Christians from the discomfort and the lament. The end goal may be the stirring up of faith, but the means to that end is an unintentional triumphalism. This narrative can leave us blindly optimistic rather than soberly prayerful.

I am thankful for those of you who have read these words and sought the Lord. This, in all of its beautiful simplicity, should be our response. We must seek Him for help, and He is eager and joyfully pleased to help us.

This remains my greatest hope and deepest encouragement. The Father, who loves us in ways that are beyond our imagination, is definitely at work. His work is perfect. He is helping us to be ready for the days to come, as well as for the days that are already upon us. There is no one like Him. I am beyond awed and utterly thankful that He is in charge.

I want to give you two final glimpses into our future before we go. The first is found in Paul's letter to the Ephesians:

> And He Himself gave some to be apostles, some prophets, some evangelists, and some pastors and teachers, for the equipping of the saints for the work of ministry, for the edifying of the body of Christ, till we all come to the unity of the faith and of the knowledge of the Son of God, to a perfect man, to the measure of the stature of the fullness of Christ; that we should no longer be children, tossed to and fro and carried about with every wind of doctrine, by the trickery of men, in the cunning craftiness of deceitful plotting, but, speaking the truth in love, may grow up in all things into Him who is the head—Christ—from whom the whole body, joined and knit together by what every joint supplies, according to the effective working by which

every part does its share, causes growth of the body for the edifying of itself in love.

Ephesians 4:11–16

This is our future: the family of God—from every tribe, tongue, nation, denomination and cultural background—coming into the unity of the faith and the knowledge of Jesus, so that we can be fully mature in Him and filled with love for one another. Before this race is over, we are really going to enjoy and celebrate one another with no more strife, comparison or competition.

Finally, I leave you with this:

And I heard, as it were, the voice of a great multitude, as the sound of many waters and as the sound of mighty thunderings, saying, "Alleluia! For the Lord God Omnipotent reigns! Let us be glad and rejoice and give Him glory, for the marriage of the Lamb has come, and His wife has made herself ready." And to her it was granted to be arrayed in fine linen, clean and bright, for the fine linen is the righteous acts of the saints. Then he said to me, "Write: 'Blessed are those who are called to the marriage supper of the Lamb!'" And he said to me, "These are the true sayings of God."

Revelation 19:6–9

Amen.

NOTES

Chapter 1 Preparing to Engage in the Future Now

1. Martin Luther King Jr., "Where Do We Go From Here?," speech to the Southern Christian Leadership Conference, Atlanta, Georgia, August 16, 1967.

Chapter 2 Divine Justice and the Return of Jesus

1. Fred R. Shapiro, *The Yale Book of Quotations* (New Haven, Conn.: Yale University Press, 2006), 724.

2. John Keegan, *The First World War* (New York: Knopf Doubleday, 2000), 9–10.

3. See Daniel 7:25; 8:23; Matthew 24:9–13; 2 Timothy 3:1–9; Revelation 17:6.

Chapter 3 Three Storms That Will Change the World

1. Revelation 17–18 expands on these ideas, but it is important to note that these chapters are built around a significant number of Old Testament prophecies, such as Isaiah 13–14; 21:1–10; 43:14–17; 46–48; Jeremiah 50–51; Daniel 11:21–45; and Zechariah 5.

2. Revelation 9:20–21 would be a key example of a portrayal of the culture of wickedness that takes root in the days before the coming of the Lord.

3. Arthur Wallis, *In the Day of Thy Power: The Scriptural Principles of Revival* (Fort Washington, Penn.: CLC Publications, 2010), 23.

4. Ibid., 27.

5. Adapted from a lecture by David Pawson, "Romans 1:18–31, Part 1, A507, *Romans*" (Hudson, Mass.: Good Seed Ministries, n.d.), http://www.goodseed.org.

Chapter 4 The Coming Storm of Revival

1. See, for example, 1 Samuel 2:8; Daniel 7:13–14, 21, 27; Matthew 5:5; Matthew 19:14.

2. See John 3:29; 2 Corinthians 11:2; Ephesians 5:31–32; Revelation 19:7–9; Revelation 21:2, 9–11.

3. See Genesis 31:8; Numbers 11:17; Judges 6:34; 14:6; 15:4; 1 Chronicles 28:12.

4. Other passages speak of this as well, for example, Revelation 6:12–17.

5. See Matthew 23:37–39; 24:14; Luke 18:1–8.

Chapter 5 The Coming Storm of Rage

1. See, for example, Psalm 46:6; Isaiah 26:20–21; 34:1–17; Jeremiah 25:15–38; Zechariah 14:1–3.

2. See Psalm 2:7.

3. See Psalm 72:15; Isaiah 11:1–2.

4. See 1 Thessalonians 5:3.

5. See Psalm 12.

6. I am taking the term *vengeance* from 2 Thessalonians 1:7–10, which reads in part, "when the Lord Jesus is revealed from heaven with His mighty angels, in flaming fire taking vengeance on those who do not know God, and on those who do not obey the gospel of our Lord Jesus Christ. These shall be punished with everlasting destruction from the presence of the Lord and from the glory of His power, when He comes, in that Day, to be glorified in His saints and to be admired among all those who believe."

7. See Revelation 3:12; 21:2, 9–10, 22; 2 Timothy 2:4.

Chapter 6 The Coming Storm of Political and Economic Disruption

1. See Acts 19:18–19. If, as some have speculated, they burned books that were worth 50,000 silver talents rather than silver denarii, then they burned the equivalent of 1.5 billion dollars of sorcery books.

2. As Jesus famously stated, where our treasures are, there will our hearts be also (see Matthew 6:21).

Chapter 7 The Birth of Cultural Narrative

1. Glenn S. Sunshine, *Why You Think the Way You Do: The Story of the Western Worldviews from Rome to Home* (Grand Rapids, Mich.: Zondervan, 2009), 114.

2. Descartes's statement can be contrasted with the biblical point of view as expressed by the apostle Paul: "In Him we live and move and have our being" (Acts 17:28). The writer of Hebrews stated that all things are upheld by the word of His power (see Hebrews 1:3).

3. Sunshine, 129.

4. G. K. Chesterton, "Anti-Religious Thought in the Eighteenth Century" in *The Spice of Life and Other Essays* (out of print but published on the website of The Society of Gilbert Keith Chesterton, 2019, https://www.chesterton.org/anti-religious-thought).

5. In this regard, Voltaire was an early voice feeding into an expression of Psalm 2 within Europe that has great relevance for us to remember in our own day.

6. Steven Nadler, "Baruch Spinoza," *The Stanford Encyclopedia of Philosophy*, Spring 2019 edition, edited by Edward N. Zalta, https://plato.stanford.edu/archives/spr2019/entries/spinoza/.

Chapter 8 The Modern Expression of the Cultural Narrative

1. Rogier Creemers, ed., "Planning Outline for the Construction of a Social Credit System (2014–2020)," China Copyright and Media, posted June 14, 2014 and updated April, 25, 2015, https://chinacopyrightandmedia.wordpress.com/2014/06/14/planning-outline-for-the-construction-of-a-social-credit-system-2014-2020/ (from the government document: "State Council Notice Concerning Issuance of the Planning Outline for the Construction of a Social Credit System (2014–2020)").

2. Amanda Lee, "China's Credit System Stops the Sale of over 26 Million Plane and Train Tickets," *South China Morning Post*, April 18, 2019, https://www.scmp.com/economy/china-economy/article/3006763/chinas-social-credit-system-stops-sale-over-26-million-plane.

3. Gustavo Gutiérrez, *The God of Life* (Maryknoll, N.Y.: Orbis, 1991), 112.

4. Stephen Thomas Kirschner, "Cultural Marxism: The Origins of the Present-Day Social Justice Movement, and Political Correctness," The Policy, February 14, 2017, https://thepolicy.us/cultural-marxism-the-origins-of-the-present-day-social-justice-movement-and-political-correctness-ffb89c6ef4f1.

5. Ibid.

6. Ibid.

Chapter 9 The Way of Victory and Redemption

1. See Matthew 16:1–4; 24:32–44; Luke 19:41–44; 21:34–36.

2. See Matthew 24:36, 42–44, 50; 25:13; Mark 13:33–38; Luke 21:36; Revelation 16:15.

3. See 2 Corinthians 1:21; 1 John 2:20, 27.

4. See Galatians 1:4; 1 Corinthians 1:20; 2:6–8; 2 Corinthians 4:4; Ephesians 2:2; Titus 2:12.

Chapter 10 Preparing the Next Generation

1. See Matthew 18:3; Mark 10:15; Luke 18:16.

2. Sanctus Augustinus, *Enarratio in Psalmum* 72, 1: CCL 39, 986 (PL 36, 914).

3. Andrew Fletcher, *An Account of a Conversation concerning a Right Regulation of Governments for the common Good of Mankind in a Letter to the Marquiss of Montrose, the Earls of Rothes, Roxburg and Haddington, From London the first of December, 1703* (Farmington Hills, Mich.: Gale ECCO eighteenth century collections, [print edition, 2010], originally published in Edinburgh, 1704), n.p.

4. A. W. Tozer, *Knowledge of the Holy* (New York: HarperCollins, 1978), 5.

5. See, for example, Isaiah 56:7; Amos 9:11; Acts 15:6–29; Ephesians 3:1–21; 6:18; Revelation 7:9–17.

6. This is the plan that the apostle Paul unfolded comprehensively to the Body of Christ in the book of Ephesians.

David Sliker has been a senior leader at the International House of Prayer missions base in Kansas City, Missouri, for the past eighteen years. Serving with his wife, Tracey, and their four children, Riley, Lauren, Daniel and Finney, David's primary ministry calling is as an intercessor. Additionally, he teaches internationally, equipping saints in prayer, the power of the Holy Spirit, passion for the Word of God and the proclamation of Jesus' return. He is the vice-president of the International House of Prayer University, where he teaches about prayer and intimacy with Jesus, missions, biblical studies and the return of Jesus. He is the author of *End-Times Simplified: Preparing Your Heart for the Coming Storm* (revised edition, Forerunner Publishing, 2013).